MEMOIR OF A PILGRIMAGE FOR EIGHT

Memoir of a

PILGRIMAGE
FOR EIGHT

Val-des-Choues *to* **Pluscarden Abbey**

PHILLIP C. ADAMO

split
infin-
itive

BOOKS

Split Infinitive Books, LLC
3220 Cedar Avenue South
Minneapolis, Minnesota 55407
USA

Imprint: Lulu.com

ISBN: 978-1-716-57797-0

For Noel, first of the Pluscarden 1230
pilgrims to reach the heavenly Jerusalem

For the monks and the pilgrims

And for David

Royal Patron

Her Royal Highness Princess Michael of Kent

Patrons

Rory Stewart, OBE
Author of *The Places in Between*

Alice Carter (née Warrender)
Author of *An Accidental Jubilee*

Harry Bucknall
Author of *Like a Tramp, Like a Pilgrim*

Contents

Foreword   v

Prologue   1

Introduction   3

Chapters

    1—Val-des-Choues to Val-Croissant   11
    2—Val-Croissant to Brienne-le-Château   28
    3—Brienne-le-Château to Laon   39
    4—Laon to Thérouanne   52
    5—Thérouanne to London   59
    6—London to Prinknash   70
    7—Prinknash to Melton Mowbray   79
    8—Melton Mowbray to Ampleforth   88
    9—Ampleforth to Alnwick Castle   97
    10—Alnwick Castle to Edinburgh   105
    11—Edinburgh to Luss   112
    12—Luss to Stratherrik   119
    13—Stratherrik to Pluscarden   130

Postscript   147

Acknowledgements   151

Foreword

The spirit of medieval monks from Val-des-Choues survives in the remains of the monasteries they built, such as the one inhabited by modern monks at Pluscarden. The Valliscaulian Order is an interesting object of academic study. Phil Adamo is a master historian and a skilled teacher of this subject. He is also a long-standing friend of the monks at Pluscarden—over the years he has brought groups of his students from across the seas to visit the Abbey.

So it was that when we planned the '1230 Pilgrimage' we enlisted Phil's help and entrusted him with compiling a record of it. The following pages are Phil's personal memoir of the pilgrimage. Informative, amusing and deeply moving by turns, Phil takes us on his own spiritual journey in the midst of continual physical and emotional challenges, introducing us to his fellow pilgrims and others he encounters along the way.

The trek from Val-des-Choues to Pluscarden was more than a fund-raising exercise. It was a true pilgrimage. The walkers became pilgrims because they depended on the mercy of others, and on being merciful to one another. They allowed their lives to be interrupted and embraced a way of life that they could not control individually. During their journey, they became a community.

We at Pluscarden are grateful to Phil and all who made the walk. The pilgrims' experience strengthened our sense of fellowship with the monasteries and other Christian communities that provided them with nightly shelter. It also renewed the connection between our monastery and its place of origin.

— Abbot Anselm Atkinson, OSB

Prologue

1193   Monastery of Val-des-Choues founded by a hermit in a remote valley in Burgundy.

1230   Pluscarden Abbey founded in northern Scotland as a daughter house of Val-des-Choues.

2000   Researching Pluscarden, I was charmed by the monks who work and pray there. This would be the first of many visits.

2015   Received an email that would change my life …

> Dear Professor Adamo,
>
> I have been charged with raising £5 million for the Pluscarden Abbey South Range Project (a new build on old foundations). Details attached. Clearly UK lottery funding and the seeking out of private donors and charities will be my aim, but events will also play a role. One I have come up with is a pilgrimage to replicate the original journey made from Burgundy, by the Valliscaulians, to Pluscarden …
>
> Interestingly, the distance is 1088.2 miles and would make a spectacular pilgrimage (I would up this to 1230 to fit in with the birth of Pluscarden!). It would be a major project, but I believe worth pursuing, perhaps setting off from Lugny in a year's time.
>
> Brother Michael de Klerk at Pluscarden said that you were the expert on the Valliscaulians and I hoped that you might be able to give me more background, advice, and help with this ambitious project!!
>
> With very kind regards and I look forward to hearing from you,
> David Broadfoot

David and I met at the Hotel Ivanhoe in Rome and in two days we mapped out the pilgrimage route—1300 miles in 13 weeks. It was our attempt to recreate the path of the monks who in the year 1230 journeyed north from Val-des-Choues and eventually founded Pluscarden Abbey in Moray, near Elgin, Scotland. We also included some side trips to sites of historic and/or spiritual interest.

2017   The Pluscarden 1230 Pilgrimage became a reality. It was at once a historical reconstruction, a fundraiser, a public relations event, a physical challenge, and a spiritual journey. This book tells some of what happened along the way.

Apologia

Medieval authors, especially theologians and historians, often included an *apologia*, an explanation of what they were attempting to do, as a kind of insurance against accusations of heresy, or insults to the crown that might get them beheaded.

Here's mine.

This book attempts to capture the many memories, good and ill, that I experienced on the Pluscarden 1230 Pilgrimage. My memory isn't perfect. And even if it were, this would still be a biased record, seen through my lens, expressing my singular and perhaps quirky point of view. I've freely commented on the people and places I encountered along the way, as I saw and experienced them in the moment, and tried to do this sincerely and honestly, without malice. I did my best to observe and comment on myself just as honestly.

If nothing else, a pilgrimage, like a life, should be a quest for truth. You can judge for yourself if I've landed anywhere near there. All I can say is that I've given it my best effort.

Introduction

Patience is more worthy than miracle-working.

—Margery Kempe, pilgrim and mystic,
from the *Book of Margery Kempe* (c. 1430)

What is a pilgrimage?

This was a question that occupied our thoughts on an almost daily basis during our walk from Val-des-Choues to Pluscarden. What is a pilgrimage? And, depending on the answer, are we *really* doing a pilgrimage or is this just some sort of pleasant walking holiday?

The practice of pilgrimage has its roots in religion and spirituality. It usually involves a journey (sometimes a very long journey), often with the goal of visiting a religious shrine or other location of great spiritual power. The person who makes such a journey is called a pilgrim.

Obscure etymology alert:

> The Latin *peregrinus* (pilgrim) comes from the prefix *per*, "beyond," and the root *agri/ager*, "country, land, field." Hence a pilgrim was literally someone "from beyond the country," i.e., a foreigner.

Pilgrimage has existed in many cultures throughout history: Christians traveling to Jerusalem, Muslims making the *hajj* to Mecca, Hindus on their way to Varanasi. Modern-day pilgrimage often emphasizes these historical roots. Pilgrims on the Camino de

Santiago today recreate a route that is at least 900 years old. Another aspect of pilgrimage, at least in the medieval Christian tradition, includes a kind of penance, the hardship of walking great distances acting as satisfaction for sins committed earlier.

Was the Pluscarden 1230 Pilgrimage a pilgrimage in any of those senses?

For starters, it was only loosely historical. The premise of the Pluscarden 1230 Pilgrimage was based on the idea that Val-des-Choues in Burgundy sent monks to Scotland to found Pluscarden. Were we accurately recreating their journey?

Well, no.

First, we have no written record from the 13th-century monks who left Val-des-Choues for Scotland. Did they travel the whole way on foot? On horseback? By ship? Their sponsor, Scottish King Alexander II, could easily have provided any of these means of transportation. But did he?

We also have no idea which path they took, by land or by sea. We can guess that those long-ago monks probably went in as straight a line as possible: from Val-des-Choues to Calais to Dover, then from Dover to Morayshire, to the future site of Pluscarden.

The route of the Pluscarden 1230 Pilgrimage wasn't so simple, at least not in terms of being the shortest, most direct path. For example, our "re-constructed" pilgrimage began by heading south, for no other reason than we wished to visit Val-des-Choues's other daughter monasteries—Val-Saint-Benoît and Val-Croissant—along the way.

And in the UK, instead of going from Dover straight up the east coast to Pluscarden, we cut west from London across to Prinknash, the Benedictine monastery that gave a new foundation to modern-day Pluscarden. From there we headed northeast again to Edinburgh, then west again to Ardchattan, another daughter house of Val-des-Choues, near Oban. Next we headed north and east again, visiting Beauly, a third daughter of Val-des-Choues in Scotland, before finally arriving at Pluscarden. All of this zig-zagging would have made no sense to our medieval counterparts.

But for the Pluscarden 1230 pilgrims, it meant the chance for deeper experiences: visiting the great cathedrals at Reims, Laon, and Westminster; connecting to other monastic communities; even enjoying spiritual experiences not connected to organized religion, like hiking through the Scottish Highlands, whose immense beauty makes a strong case for God's existence.

Was Pluscarden 1230 a real a pilgrimage?

Medieval pilgrims, having hiked 15 to 20 miles a day, acquired lodging or set up camp wherever they found themselves, only to break camp from that same spot the next morning and continue on their way.

We didn't do that.

First, not everyone walked the entire way. We had two and sometimes three support vehicles. Some of our pilgrims rode in cars, at least some of the way. And throughout the walk, we made compromises for our larger group.

Sidenote on numbers:

> Many pilgrims came and went over the course of thirteen weeks: 20 to 25 per week at the high end, 8 at the low end, a core group that made the entire journey.

Traveling in larger numbers had advantages, like safety and companionship. But traveling in large numbers also had disadvantages, like finding suitable group accommodations. On some days we walked right into the lodgings the support team had organized. Other days, we were picked up at the edge of a forest and driven a good forty-five minutes to a church basement in some village, the closest lodging that could be found for a group of our size. The whole thing may feel less romantic, hearing it described like this. In truth, it lessened some of the challenges of the trip, but this does not mean the trip was challenge free.

Let me give you an idea of a typical day.

Mornings

Rise early. The earlier the better because you want to put some miles behind you before the sun gets too high. Wash up. Eat breakfast. Sort your lunch for that day, usually sandwiches and fruit. On a lucky day, the cooks will have purchased tins of sardines with various sauces. Water. Do not forget to take water, though if you do, cemeteries often have spigots with potable water. Keep an eye out.

Pack your day bag. Don't forget your map, which you should have prepared the night before. Don't be one of those pilgrims who waits until that morning to prepare the day's map. Be sure to bring your rain gear, hat, and walking stick. Bring your journal if you're journaling and remember your *fully-charged* cell phone, which you will need when you have to call the support team to tell them you're lost.

"Never say you are lost," the support team will tell you. "You are geographically embarrassed." This is meant to make you feel better.

Attend Mass, which will be over by the departure time of 7am. Look around and see that there are only two or three of you besides the priest. Oh, well.

Pack your sleeping bag and other kit and leave these next to the entry of the lodging. On this particular morning, you are being driven to the starting point at the edge of a forest. Do not be late or your lateness will cause everyone else to get a late start.

The walk

Start out as a group. Look at your maps. You did remember to bring your map, didn't you? Review any peculiarities of the route. Review the meeting point, sometimes called the RV or *rendezvous* point. Note the pick-up time. Have you packed enough water?

The group departs. Within minutes, the fast walkers have disappeared from view. You are a slow walker and you've learned not to be bothered by this. Set your own pace. Appreciate the sights and sounds of wherever you are. Be present. You are not in the middle of whatever soul-crushing job you perform to pay the rent. You are on a pilgrimage: a beautiful, difficult, sweaty, but ultimately spiritually regenerating pilgrimage. Relish it!

Enjoy the company of the other walkers who have agreed to walk with you, at least for a while. Have lunch whenever you get hungry, preferably on the banks of a river, or on the seashore, or in the shade of a parish churchyard.

Continue your walk and try to take in everything. Or take in nothing. Sometimes zoning out is just the ticket. Arrive on time at the RV point. Even though you're the slowest walker, you are not the last one to arrive because someone didn't bring their map and got lost. Board the van and enjoy a brief bit of air conditioning as you're driven to the new lodging for that night.

Evenings

Arrive at the lodging and immediately scramble for a good spot to set up your sleeping bag. This is critical. If you brought a tent, or even if you didn't bring a tent and it's possible to sleep outside, do so. Sleeping outside isn't always possible or advised. The most safety and relative comfort comes from sleeping in the large church hall or basement that the local parish has donated to the pilgrims for the night. These are nothing more than big open rooms. You'll want to claim a space next to a wall, preferably two walls in a corner. You don't want to have people crawling over you for their late-night visits to the loo. You especially do not want to sleep next to the loo. You may get lucky and find yourself in a church hall with an extra loo, one that is especially clean and odor free with a lock on its door. Should you find yourself in this situation, consider sleeping in the loo. If you're exhausted and need some alone time, this will feel like a private room with its own *en suite* toilet. Finally, you will want to identify the snorers, or have them self-identify. Sleep as far away from the snorers as you can. If you remembered to bring ear plugs, use them—not all snorers know that they snore. Whatever you do, stake out your sleeping space as soon as you arrive.

If there are showers available, take one. You never know if the next place will have showers or not, so take a shower whenever you can. You'll feel more relaxed and your fellow pilgrims will thank you.

Sometimes people from the local parish will have prepared dinner for the pilgrims, but most often the pilgrimage cooks have cooked for you. When dinner is served, enjoy the good company of your fellow pilgrim. Share the stories of your day's adventures and listen to theirs. As routine as the days can seem, there are always adventures to share. Almost every evening has a meeting to discuss how things are going, food requests, and at the very least to copy maps for the next day's hike. This "copying of maps" consists of grabbing one of the color-copies of a topographic map provided and tracing the designated route from the master map with a yellow or orange highlighter. Remember to indicate the mile markers, so that, should you become ill or injured, you can call the support staff and tell them where to pick you up.

There's always time for socializing before bed, but many pilgrims turn in right away, so try to respect the noise levels. Just before you hit the sack, you can also use the expensive head torch you bought at the camping store to do some reading. One last trip to the loo and, Bob's your uncle, that was your day.

Get up tomorrow and do it all over again.

This description of the daily routine must sound quite tedious, which I suppose it was. The most interesting part of the pilgrimage (for me at least), was all the human interaction that happened beyond this routine. Now that you know the tedious bits, we need never speak of them again. One last thing before you fall asleep. Tomorrow morning, before you head out, be sure your kit is neatly packed and leave it by the entrance to the church hall, lest the support staff forget to put your luggage in the van for transport to the next lodging.

Wait.

Did I just say that the pilgrims' luggage was transported in a van? Didn't we carry it on our backs?!

This is *not* a real pilgrimage!

Fans of the Camino de Santiago, in particular, will be appalled by this fact. My understanding is that "true pilgrims" on the Camino carry their own luggage and that only true pilgrims are offered first dibs on the limited lodgings along the way.

In fairness, some of the Pluscarden pilgrims were shocked that their luggage would be carried for them in a van. I, for one, had purchased a posh, new rucksack, exclusively for this trip, and had practiced packing and unpacking it until it was just right. I even practiced carrying it around on my own back to see how that would go. But I must honestly admit that, when I discovered this magical "luggage in the van for transport" service, I did not resist.

At this point, if you feel the need to judge us for all the ways we did not live up to your vision of a "real" pilgrimage (walking every step, cooking our own grub, carrying our own rucksacks), well, go ahead. If your disappointment is unbearable, you may stop reading here. But I hope you can tolerate and forgive our shortcomings, for there is a remarkable story to be told, and I hope to tell it to you.

Before I begin, some praise is due our amazing support team. The Pluscarden 1230 Pilgrimage could not have happened without them.

First, Abbot Anselm and all of the monks at Pluscarden, as well as the countless friends and family, who were not on the pilgrimage, but who prayed for our health and safety and our eternal souls. Counted among this group are the many communities and individuals who gave us food and shelter along the way.

David directed the entire project from a tiny office in Elgin, with administrative aid from Alison. David was also constantly on the road, driving ahead of the pilgrims to secure lodgings— sometimes for the same day! Jai was in charge of day-to-day operations. From his trusty Land Rover, he kept us on task, made sure we always remembered to bring water, helped us understand our maps, found us when we got lost, and lovingly teased us, most often with the phrase "bloody pilgrims!" spoken in his Nepalese accent. Over the course of thirteen weeks, we had three cooks who shopped for us and prepared our dinners. Pete cooked for five weeks on the French leg of the trip. Ann and Jo took over in the kitchen for the eight weeks of the UK leg. Jo also drove one of the vans, as did Tomasz (who was also our mechanic), while we were in France.

Some of the Pluscarden monks traveled with us and helped the support team with a variety of tasks, the aforementioned Brother Michael in particular. Some of these monks were also priests—Father Giles in France, Fathers Martin and Mark in the UK—who offered daily Mass for any of the pilgrims who wished to attend. The monks also provided sacraments like confession, a good sense of humor, and sometimes ice cream, critical elements for helping any pilgrimage run more smoothly.

And this was indeed, in all of the most important ways, a pilgrimage.

1

Val-des-Choues *to* Val-Croissant

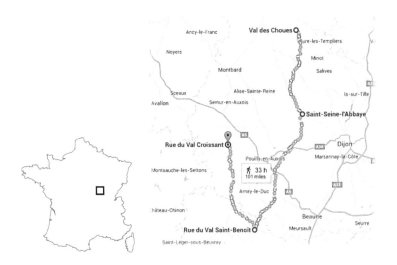

2 June

I arrive at Val-des-Choues. I've been here a couple of times before, doing research, but the sense of excitement I have now doesn't compare. This is going to be one of those moments—and by "moments" I mean the entire summer—where experiences and thoughts and feelings rush in so fast that it will be difficult to keep them organized.

As other pilgrims show up and I start to meet them, it's impossible not to think of Chaucer's pilgrims, with their varied backgrounds and ages and reasons for taking their journey. An

eighteen-year-old New Yorker named Andres—"call me Andy"—
has been sent on the pilgrimage by his mother to "straighten him
out." He seems just as goofy and unfocused as many of my students
back home. We'll see how this works out for him. There's a grad
student in film named Chris, who's joined the pilgrimage with the
hope of making a documentary about the experience. There's a
Scottish bagpiper named Iain and his American mother, Jane, from
my adopted home state of Minnesota, and a dozen-and-a-half more.

L'Abbaye du Val-des-Choues, Villiers-le-Duc.

As I settle in at Val-des-Choues, it strikes me how many people
I had to trust in order to leave my life behind for three months: the
house sitter, the dog sitter, the yard guy, my bank. Such an
undertaking is fraught with inevitable mistakes, miscommunication,
and just a hint of impending chaos. The right coping attitude is
going to be essential—not certain I can pull it off. Being
surrounded by all these other people, I'll need to find "alone time"
to recharge.

3 June

I ride with Pete to the *supermarché* to get groceries for dinner, the first of many such trips we'll take together. Pete is the cook on the five-week, French leg of the journey. He uses Scottish slang and calls our shopping trips "getting the messages." Pete desperately wants to learn French. I'm fluent, but Pete doesn't want my help when speaking with others, wants to try it on his own, which I admire. He makes lots of hand gestures and imitates the nasal sounds made by the butcher and the baker and to my surprise this seems to work.

Pete has his own culinary tastes, as do I, and our regular shopping trips find each of us trying to sway the other in what kind of food we should buy. On one of these excursions, Pete asks me to get some of the "regular cheese" and "regular bread," by which he means cheddar and mushy white bread.

"Pete," I say. "We're in France, a country that's world famous for its cheese and bread. Let's take advantage of that."

"Aye, Phillip," he says. "But this is what Scottish people like."

Really? I think to myself and suddenly feel snooty. But surely some Scottish people on this pilgrimage will prefer, or at least enjoy something fancier. (My Lord, I'm a *cheese* snob!) In fairness, Pete has to shop for the pilgrimage within a budget, which doesn't leave much room for extravagance. In lieu of debate, I buy the cheese and bread I like out of my own pocket and share it with whomever is interested.

Back at Val-des-Choues, Chris is practicing flying a drone with a small camera attached that he wants to use in his filmmaking. As Pete and I return from shopping, the drone is stuck high in a tree in the monastery's front courtyard. People are throwing sticks to try to get it down, without any luck, though their attempts are almost hypnotic. A young Frenchman who cares for the hounds at Val-des-Choues (did I mention that the former monastery is now used as a hunting lodge?), this guy goes to get a football (soccer ball for Americans) and kicks it into the air toward the drone. Two tries and it's down, unharmed. Small miracles.

I go to bed early. It's pitch black outside. Val-des-Choues sits in a valley and there's no nearby town to give off light pollution. We can see a million stars in the sky. The sound of bats chirping in the night sounds like herds of cattle wearing cowbells running down the road. I sleep well, but I wake with a big, itchy bite in a place that's hard to scratch and even more difficult to see. Spider? Bed bugs?

4 June

M. Monot, the proprietor at Val-des-Choues, donates a stone from the ruins of the old church, which the pilgrims will carry back to Pluscarden for use as the cornerstone of the new building. Mass is scheduled for 11am, in a tent across from where the monastery's church once stood. Pluscarden's abbot, Father Anselm, has driven down from Scotland to celebrate the Mass for Pentecost Sunday. He wears red vestments, symbolizing the fire of burning charity!

After Mass, we hold our first briefing to prepare for the next day's departure. David asks me to give some of Val-des-Choues's history, but to keep it brief. I'm amazed by how poorly my ego takes his request for brevity. I suppose when you've been studying something for as long as I've been studying these monks, you delude yourself that people will clamber to hear everything you've learned, but in your heart of hearts, you know this isn't true. Following the briefing, Brother Michael asks me to give a group tour of the monastery sometime that afternoon. Ego assuaged.

5 June

The weather on this first day is perfect: sunny and cool in the morning, comfortable by afternoon. Father Anselm blesses the stone from Val-des-Choues as well as all the pilgrims before we take off. Iain, youngest chieftain of his clan, dressed in full kilt and tartan, plays his bagpipes as he leads us out the doors of Val-des-Choues. The pipes must be audible in Essarois, the next village over. Leaving the front gates of the old abbey, Iain turns right and heads down the road.

Within seconds, David, dauntless organizer of our endeavor, attempts to shout above the drone of the pipes. Others soon take up his cry. We have to get Iain to stop and turn around. He's heading east, in the wrong direction!

Auspicious beginnings.

Pluscarden 1230 pilgrims, week 1.

The range of costumes on that first day deserves a word or two. I've already mentioned Iain in his kilt. In fact, after accompanying us in the right direction for half an hour or so, he runs back to Val-des-Choues and changes into more sensible hiking clothes. Angus, a forester from the village of Pluscarden, near the abbey in Scotland, sports a tweed blazer with a bowtie and a wide-brimmed, straw boatman's hat. Quite dapper. Otherwise, the pilgrims wear all manner of stiff visors and floppy hats of canvas or straw. Andy, our young American, wears a baseball cap with a camouflage design. Robbie, a sixty-ish lawyer from Scotland, wears a white brimmed golfer's hat. There are T-shirts of all colors and zip-up vests of fleece and down. Some wear shorts while others wear hiking pants that zip at the knee to convert into shorts. There are hiking boots in every price range, some worn in, others still squeaky and new enough that they're sure to cause blisters somewhere down the path. Maria, a widow in her late sixties from the Czech Republic, wears sandals without socks. Olga, a Polish hairdresser, wife of our driver/mechanic, Tomasz, wears one of the bright red T-shirts David has produced as swag for everyone on the pilgrimage. When enough of these T-shirts are gathered in one place it looks like children dressed for easy identification during a primary school outing. In spite of the T-shirt, Olga still manages to look stylish. The most sensibly dressed is Al, who wears clothing that is well-ventilated and quick drying, attire that suits a guy who's logged hundreds of miles hiking on various charity walks. Al's only accoutrement is his yellow lab, Rinnes, named for Ben Rinnes, the mountain in northern Scotland. Like Al, Rinnes walks all 1300 miles of the pilgrimage.

The most important thing to have in one's kit, in my humble opinion, is a good stick. Some of the pilgrims have fancy aluminum walking sticks with no-slip, rubber-tipped ends and foam handles for surer grip. Others have nicely-carved, wooden walking sticks that they've purchased at outdoor recreation stores, though Robbie carries one that was handed down from his father. I'm determined to find a stick along the path, an approach that seems more authentic to me. In the middle of my walking stick reverie, I spy Angus in his tweed blazer some distance from the main path, looking over some felled trees that are stacked along the forest floor. He selects a stick that seems perfectly straight—I later learn that it's ash—takes out a pocketknife and begins whittling off the stick's tiny imperfections. Nice stick, I think to myself. I can already tell, even at a distance. And a nice knife, I think. I'm already coveting two of my neighbor's belongings and the pilgrimage has only just begun. I have to get a knife, I think. Then I can cut myself the right stick.

My big lesson on this first day is how and what to pack. The answer is always "Less stuff, more water!" All day long, I carry a big, chunky sweater in my rucksack that I never use—could have dedicated some of that space to water. Tomorrow, I hope the packing will go differently.

Medieval pilgrimages often centered around visiting relics: the bones of dead saints, etc. The Pluscarden 1230 Pilgrimage transports its own relics. One of these is the stone from the ruins at Val-des-Choues, which M. Monot has given to the monks. Someone has given the pilgrims two knit dolls "dressed as pilgrims." The idea is to photograph them along the route and post their pictures to social media. The novelty of both of these ideas soon wears off. The stone turns out to be quite heavy, and while it is indeed carried by the pilgrims from Burgundy to Scotland, most of the carrying takes place in the Land Rover that accompanies the walkers. The knit dolls get lost or abandoned somewhere by the second or third week.

There is also a medieval coin bearing the image of Henry III. It was found at Pluscarden and brought to France as a gift to M. Monot, who's sending it back to Pluscarden on foot (via my pocket) and plans to retrieve it when he visits Pluscarden for the blessing of the stone, above. It's a little hokey, but also kind of wonderful.

I only walk 14 of the 20 miles on today's route when a car arrives to pick me up. I don't feel the least bit guilty about this, but it does show that all my preparation on the treadmill back home hasn't been enough. My feet are only slightly sore, but my legs are like rubber.

We sleep this night at Flavigny Abbey. The men enjoy a fantastic meal in the refectory with the monks. The women have to dine separately. After dinner, I give a fifteen-minute talk—really three five-minute talks on three different topics. The first is on monastic silence, an especially difficult practice at mealtime for those who are new to the concept. I also lecture a bit about Roman roads, since we're going to be walking on one the next day. Finally, I begin a discussion of medieval pilgrimage as penance. There's a nice smattering of applause when I finish. My fellow pilgrims call me "professor," in that European way that signals genuine respect—not something that often happens in the US.

After my talk, we have some map reading orientation, then it's early to bed. The mantra for the walkers is 10 by 10, i.e., 10 miles by 10am. You do not want to be stuck on a long, straight Roman road when the sun is high in the sky.

6 June

Well rested from our stay at Flavigny, we get an early start on our second day. Father Elijah and Brother Basil, two monks in their mid- to late-thirties, lead us up the hill (a 40-degree incline), from Flavigny to the start of the forest path. Once we know the way, they take off running, in their monastic habits, sprinting at a good clip like the fit young monks that they are. Already panting and only halfway up the hill, I'm not sure whether to be impressed or jealous. I opt for impressed and hope that by the end of the summer I, too, might be in such good shape.

Thinking back, the monks may have been running back to Flavigny to avoid the downpour of rain that soon hits us. Even with rain gear, everyone gets soaked to the bone.

Our destination that evening is the village of Malain, where we have lodging in the local parish hall. The space can seat about 100 people for dinner, but with the tables and chairs still inside it's tricky for 20 of us to find room for our sleeping bags. The rain lets up just long enough for Pete, our cook, to try to set up the cooker David has transported all the way from Scotland. I say "try to set up the cooker" because this does not happen on that evening, or for several evenings to come.

A few words about logistics. Except for the monks and I, the Pluscarden 1230 Pilgrimage was led by former military men. David, the pilgrimage director, retired as a Lt. Colonel after 32 years serving in the Gordon Highlanders. Jai, the operations manager, is a native of Nepal who spent over 30 years in the British Brigade of Gurkhas, ending his military career as Regimental Administrative Officer of the 1st Battalion of the Royal Regiment of Scotland. Al, our navigator, is a retired Air Commodore with the RAF—the equivalent of a one-star general. Even Pete, the cook, has done many tours in the kitchens of the Royal Marines. These were highly skilled, supremely competent men.

This is why the story of the cooker is so ironic!

I say this now, long after the events of that evening in Malain, with all the humor and love and respect I can muster. But that evening, with soaking wet clothes, an aching body, and the promise of no dinner before I settle into my sleeping bag on a hard concrete floor, I'm sure I feel none of those emotions.

It was David's idea to bring the UK-made cooker down from Scotland. It was also his idea *not* to bring any fuel for the cooker, since, hey, "we can just get a tank of butane in France." One can indeed purchase butane in France. It comes in portable storage tanks that look almost exactly like the tanks one can purchase in the UK. The one important difference is that the ones from France don't connect with the cookers from the UK. Adapters to make this happen are also not readily available. In spite of the many fine advances brought about by the European Union since 1993, the Franco-Anglo-cooker-connector problem has not been solved. So, there's food, and hungry people to eat that food, but no way to cook it.

Then it starts to rain.

As a village, Malain is charming, but too small to have a restaurant that's still open after 6pm on a Tuesday. Jai finds a pizza place in the next town over, only 30 minutes away. That's 30 minutes to drive there, 30 minutes to make enough pizza for 20 people, and 30 minutes to drive back to Malain. What else can we do? The cooker isn't working.

And this is how "story time" came to the Pluscarden 1230 Pilgrimage.

Because I'm a nerdy, medieval history professor, I bring with me on my pilgrimage the greatest book about pilgrims ever written, Chaucer's *Canterbury Tales*, in a modern English translation. For those unfamiliar, Chaucer tells the story of several pilgrims as they travel to Canterbury to visit the shrine of the martyr Thomas

Becket. In a pub where they've all gathered pre-departure, they agree to a story-telling contest. Each pilgrim will tell a story as they ride together and the winner of the contest will have the others buy him dinner. Without streaming movies on smart phones, this is what medieval people did for fun. The stories that Chaucer's characters tell range from heroic to moralistic to bawdy. There is truly something for everyone.

We're packed into the parish hall in the tiny village of Malain. It's pouring rain outside. No one has showered, everyone is tired and hungry, and pizza is 90 minutes away. Time for some diversion therapy. I take out my copy of *Canterbury Tales* and begin to read to the group from the General Prologue, in which Chaucer introduces all the characters in his story.

> A KNIGHT there was, and what a gentleman,
> Who from the moment that he first began
> To ride about the world, loved chivalry,
> Truth, honour, freedom and all courtesy

As I read this line, I notice that people are looking at Al, the Air Commodore. After only a couple of days together, people seem to recognize in him the qualities of Chaucer's knight. Interesting, I think.

> A MONK there was, one of the finest sort,

Everyone turns to Father Giles, the monk from Pluscarden.

A lawyer and a cook? Chaucer's collection of pilgrims has both of these and so do we, in Robbie and Pete. A "doctor of medicine"? We have a dentist named John. A sheriff? Ours is a spry retiree named Noel. A forester? Yes. Of all things, our 21st-century pilgrimage has a forester, none other than the dapper Angus, with his hand-crafted walking stick.

One of the most colorful characters in Chaucer's work is the Wife of Bath, a widow who has been married five times, whose face is "red of hue" from all the sun she's gotten traveling on pilgrimage.

Three times she'd travelled to Jerusalem;
And many a foreign stream she'd had to stem;
At Rome she'd been, and she'd been in Boulogne,
In Spain at Santiago, and at Cologne.
She could tell much of wandering by the way.

All eyes turn toward Maria, who walks in sandals. Maria is indeed a widow, though I think she's only had two husbands. And she is, in fact, a kind of semi-professional pilgrim, who has undertaken many famous pilgrimages, including the Camino de Santiago.

This is spooky, but also fun and fascinating. The modern pilgrims are seeing each other and themselves in this medieval collection of stories, and, consequently, as part of a historical tradition. Just as I'm reveling in all my pedagogical glory, the pizza arrives and the magic spell is broken. My fellow pilgrims eat like ravenous wolves.

7 June

All around me there's a pleasing chaos as pilgrims hustle to make tea and eat breakfast, pack their kits, and gather energy for the walk. You can sense a shift in the mood. Even after sleeping the night on cold concrete, people are excited for the day.

Angus has left his walking stick leaning against the wall outside the parish hall. Everyone who passes takes note.

"Nice stick."

"Good stick."

"Just the right height."

My feet are wrecked. I'm hobbling around like a toddler. I'll work with the support team today, help Pete with his French as he continues to work on the cooker problem. The support staff is already feeling a bit overwhelmed. I can't say I blame them, but it hasn't been a week since we started. The cooker gets fixed through a merging and fusing of various valves and couplings. It looks like it may explode any minute, but over the next three months it never does.

Pete and I arrive at Val-des-Choues's daughter house of Val-Saint-Benoît, well ahead of the pilgrims, and begin to set up camp.

According to the foundation legend of Val-Saint-Benoît, Gauthier, lord of Sully, Savigny, and Repas, took his son Humbert to the island of Rhodes to be knighted in the Order of Saint John (the Hospitallers). On his voyage home, "barbarous Turks" attacked Gauthier's ship and imprisoned him. Fearing for his life, Gauthier vowed to God and the Virgin Mary of Val-Croissant of the Order of Val-des-Choues, that if he was able to escape from the pirates, he would found a monastery to the Blessed Virgin's honor and glory, which would become a daughter house of Val-Croissant. With the Virgin Mary on his side, Gauthier escaped. Upon returning home, he fulfilled his vow.

Gauthier called together craftsmen to build a church in front of his castle at Repas, dedicated to "our good lady of Val-Croissant," who had saved his life. According to the legend, however, this was not to be the final site of the new church. The next morning, after construction had started and for several mornings thereafter, the workmen arrived at the site only to find the stones strewn about, their work on the foundation undone. Finally, on a Sunday morning, the stones seemed to lead the workers away from the castle of Repas, into the forest, to a site roughly half a league north. An invisible hand had laid down the outline of the church, the dimensions of which were exactly the same as those for the church planned at Repas. Furthermore, the masons discovered that their hammers had been placed in the form of a cross on that spot where the Virgin wanted the altar of her church to be.

The church at the monastery of Val-Saint-Benoît, Épinac.

Pedantic historian alert:

> Some parts of the legend are what we historians call "not true."
> First, the island of Rhodes in 1236 was held by Muslim pirates
> and would not have been good place for a knighting ceremony.
> Second, lots of monasteries have foundation legends where the
> building site is "relocated according to God's wishes." But who
> cares?! The story still tells us a lot about the monks who
> founded Val-Saint-Benoît, about what they believed.

Since 1982, Carthusian nuns live at Val-Saint-Benoît, which
they have rechristened as the Monastery of Our Lady of Adoration.

There are showers here and I decide to take one before the
sweaty hordes arrive. After thoroughly soaping up, head lathered
in shampoo, the water cuts off. I put on clothes over my soapy body
and track down one of the nuns to report the water problem. She
hauls a bucket of water for me so I can properly rinse off as she
addresses the plumbing issue. Happily rinsed, I rejoin her and she

tells me how this has happened to her a few times. Discussing showering with a nun—or perhaps I should say, "with a nun, discussing showering"—I suddenly feel self-conscious. Luckily, Tomasz, our intrepid mechanic, arrives and flips a breaker switch that had caused the pump to shut down. I thank him, but his only reply is to shrug and say "I am mechanic," in his thick Polish accent. With the water problem solved, the nun and I smile at each other and she departs.

There's a Vespers service, then Mass in the priory's beautifully restored church. After Mass, about eight of the nuns bring us cakes for dessert. Iain plays his pipes. Father Giles dances a jig. The sisters of Our Lady of Adoration come from many countries, as do the pilgrims, and there is much laughing as we attempt conversations in French and Spanish and Czech and English.

A full day. A wonderful day.

8 June

We leave Val-Saint-Benoît for the village of Huilly.

This is my second day working with the support team, hoping that my feet will get better. Tomasz and Pete, a Pole and a Scot, make a hilarious team as they try to communicate. It's especially funny when Pete tries to tell a joke and has to explain it because the wordplay doesn't translate.

"A duck walks into a bar," Pete says, then continues the joke, performing both characters. "'Got any bread?' the duck asks.

"'No,' says the barman.

"Got any bread?' the duck asks again.

"'No.'

"'Got any bread?'

"'No, we've no' got any bread.'

"'Got any bread?'

"'No! We've no' got *any* effin' bread.'

"'Got any bread?'

"'Are you *deef*?! We haven't got *any* effin' bread. Ask me again and I'll nail your *effin'* beak to the bar you *irritatin'*, *effin'* bird!'

"'Got any nails?'

"'NO!'

"... 'Got any bread?'"

I laugh. Tomasz stares at Pete, expressionless.

"Why does duck want nails?' Tomasz asks. "Bread makes sense, but why duck wants nails?"

"No," Pete says. "The duck doesn't want the nails. The duck is checking to see if the barman has nails."

"Yes, I know. I not stupid. I am mechanic. But why duck asks for nails? I thought duck wants bread."

"Yes ... Well ... ah, feck it."

We set up camp in another parish hall, surrounded by streets and concrete, which means no camping and another night on a hard floor.

The pilgrims return and their spirits are high. They cackle and chirp as they set up their sleeping bags and relate the day's adventures. Young Andy lost his passport. Then he got lost. After engaging Jai for the better part of an hour, Andy remembered that he left his passport in his other bag. Everyone but Jai finds this amusing.

Andy is also the first of the group to acquire a nickname. We now call him "the Spaniel." Young Andy is quite fit and he aspires to keep up with the fast walkers. But Andy has short legs and he always falls behind on the walk except for one innovative practice: he runs ahead, then slows down, allowing the long-legged fast walkers to catch up to him. Angus finds that this behavior resembles the goofy gait of a Springer Spaniel, so Andy has become "the Spaniel." We all call him this, even to his face. He doesn't seem offended and even seems to appreciate that the "older boys" are paying attention to him.

Over dinner, Pete and Father Giles exchange many stupid and sexist jokes, with great relish. People laugh or groan or sometimes both. Chris warns people that he'll be filming his documentary in the forest where we'll be hiking tomorrow and asks that people "act natural." Then one of the pilgrims asks, "What about the story?"

The story? Yes. More of the *Canterbury Tales*? I thought this was just a one-off, a distraction for complaining stomachs, but now someone asks for another. I ask if they want me to read or just tell them one of the stories. They prefer the latter. With all the joking that's gone before, I think the "Miller's Tale" will be a good fit. It's my favorite of Chaucer's stories, so I know the outline of it by heart. The rest I make up.

For those unfamiliar, the "Miller's Tale" is the story of a lover's triangle between a carpenter's beautiful young wife, a handsome university student, and an unattractive parish clerk. The carpenter himself plays the cuckold in the tale. The humor is bawdy and includes many purloined kisses in the night. One of the clerk's kisses on the mouth turns out to be a kiss on the young wife's arse, which she has stuck out her window. The clerk, realizing something is amiss, proclaims curiously that "a woman has no beard." Nonetheless, the clerk returns for another kiss. This time the student sticks his arse out the window and farts in the clerk's face. The clerk takes revenge by retrieving a hot poker from the town blacksmith and shoving it up the student's bum.

Nothing translates across time and space like a good fart joke. My fellow pilgrims laugh and laugh.

"Can't wait to hear tomorrow's story," someone says. A pilgrimage tradition is born. Or I should say, in deference to Chaucer, reborn?

I'm happy the pilgrims like the idea of listening to stories, and I'm really happy that they seem to be asking for it on their own. I don't want this to seem programmatic.

9 June

We're staying at Val-Croissant, the first of Val-des-Choues's daughter houses, which we've already encountered in the foundation legend of Val-Saint Benoît. I've only visited here once before, but it still seems familiar.

My feet are better today, but the rest of my body is giving me trouble: fever, chills, diarrhea. Something definitely bit me on the arse at Val-des-Choues. It's not as bad as a hot poker up the bum, but its burns nonetheless and itches like crazy. I fear this may be the cause of my other symptoms.

10 June

We leave Val-Croissant and walk to the monastery of la-Pierre-qui-Vire where we'll spend the weekend. Some of this week's pilgrims will leave us. New ones will arrive. I'm very curious to see how this goes.

2

Val-Croissant *to*
Brienne-le-Château

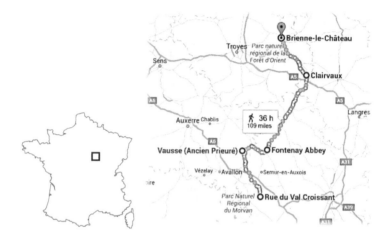

11 June

I finally rejoin the walkers and make it all the way to the Abbaye
Sainte-Marie de la Pierre-qui-Vire. The monastery is tucked into a
beautiful, dense forest. All the buildings seem more recent and I
learn that the abbey was founded in 1850. The place would be old
by American standards but is just a baby among European
monasteries. The name, Saint Mary of the Stone that Turns, refers
to a dolmen—one rock balanced on top of another—that can spin
and rotate with a simple push of the hand. The monks mounted a
statue of Our Lady atop the dolmen, hence "Saint Mary of the Stone
that Turns.

Mid-afternoon, some of the pilgrims from the first week depart and new pilgrims arrive. Among those leaving is Angus of the perfect walking stick. I rack up the nerve to ask him about this stick. Is he going to take it back to Scotland? If not, perhaps I could take care of it for him, use it, and return it at the end of the pilgrimage? He agrees and I feel like my heart will burst.

Dolmen with statue of Our Lady, Abbaye Sainte-Marie de la Pierre-qui-Vire, Saint-Léger-Vaubann.

We have a bit of a snit during dinner. The monastery has a large space for serving guests, with several sections that can be closed off to give groups privacy. Under the belief that we would want to talk, the monks have put us in one of these rooms so as not to disturb the other guests, who are practicing monastic silence during the meal. I suggest that we do the same and explain a little about why silence is so important in a monastic community. Robbie, the lawyer, objects and says flat out that he won't eat quietly, not even for 30 minutes. I leave our group and go eat in silence with the guests in the other room.

Robbie apologizes later and admits that the others in our group teased him for not being able to be silent.

Monastic life lesson alert:

> St. Basil the Great, one of the fathers of Western monasticism, said that living in community is better than living as a hermit. "As a hermit," he said, "one has no opportunity to practice Christian charity."

After dinner, I give a talk in French to the monks of la Pierre-qui-Vire. I start with a very short overview of monastic history and then put Val-des-Choues and Pluscarden in context. There are thirty monks in the audience, as well as some of our group, who introduce themselves and answer questions about the pilgrimage. Father Giles and I take turns translating.

We end the evening sitting outside the dormitories and telling jokes and getting to know the new pilgrims into the wee hours.

12 June

I wake up refreshed and ready to walk again.

It's a glorious thing to enjoy the hospitality of monks. Real beds with clean sheets. Hot showers. Simple but delicious meals. Because we've taken on more pilgrims, with more luggage than our single van can carry, the abbot at la Pierre-qui-Vire is letting us borrow one of their vans, at least until we leave France for England.

Our destination today is Vézelay, a medieval fortified town built on the side of a steep hill. Our lodging is some sort of parish school about halfway up the hill and just as I arrive I can feel that last stretch of the hike in my thighs. I decide not to worry about claiming my sleeping spot, but to venture further, to the top of the hill where Vézelay's magnificent cathedral overlooks the valley below.

The cathedral is actually attached to a monastery that was first dedicated in the 8th century, then rededicated in the 9th century by monks of the Cluniac order. Vézelay claims to hold the relics of Mary Magdalene, the ultimate penitent for Catholic believers. Perhaps for this reason, Vézelay became one of the popular starting points for the pilgrimage route to Compostela.

As with many medieval buildings that have lasted this long, Vézelay's cathedral is a mishmash of styles, from Romanesque to Gothic to 19th-century "reconstructions." I think about the notion of reconstructing history and whatever it is we're doing on this pilgrimage as I ponder the cathedral's south tympanum, the semicircular structure above the door. It was installed in 1840 by the great monument restorer, Eugène Viollet-le-Duc, the same guy who put those famous gargoyles atop the cathedral of Notre Dame in Paris. Viollet-le-Duc's Romanesque-style tympanum shows the Last Judgment, a common theme above many a cathedral door. The elongated figures he's placed there strike angular poses, perhaps showing the anxiety of the Last Judgment.

This is a good way to end the day after a long walk, contemplating the big questions of history and art and the end times. And if I hurry back down the hill, I can join some of my fellow pilgrims at the ice cream shop before it closes.

13 June

From Vézelay, we trek to Val-des-Choues's daughter house of Vausse, which has its own interesting history.

Following the Revolution of 1789, all the monasteries in France were dissolved and their land and buildings became property of the state. Vausse was sold to the Petit family and became their home. One of the grandchildren, Ernest Petit, visited Vausse every summer during his childhood. On one such visit, he observed the family servant using old scraps of parchment to cover her fruit preserves. The parchment was covered with "curious handwriting," which intrigued Ernest so much that he taught himself to read it. These turned out to be documents from the monastery's early history.

Ernest Petit (1835-1918), grew up to become one of France's most famous historians. His nine-volume history of the dukes of Burgundy is still a classic. When he inherited Vausse, Petit had an upper level built in the chapel, which became his study. At one point the study had a billiard table, on which Petit played with his many visitors. When he wasn't playing billiards, Petit also wrote about the history of his family home. From his work, we can establish the foundation date of Vausse at 1204.

The cloister at Vausse Priory, Châtel-Gérard.

We arrive at Vausse to a film crew shooting a historical drama set during the French Revolution, using the serene cloister of Vausse as their location. As we walk through the monastery gates, one by one, we're told to keep quiet so as not to disturb the filmmakers. This is not our way. We want to talk and recount the day's adventures. We want to rush into wherever we're going to sleep, to claim our spots. Most importantly, Pete wants to set up the cooker and start chopping vegetables so that dinner won't be too late. But we're foiled in all of this by the regular shouts of some assistant to the assistant director, strapped with a fancy looking headset, yelling "*Silènce!*" in French every 15 to 20 minutes to keep us in line.

Ernest Petit's grandson, M. Degouve, is the current proprietor at Vausse. He's a jolly man who claims to remember me from my earlier visit. He has invited the women pilgrims to stay in the separate house where he and his wife live. That means private rooms with sheets and hot showers for them. Jai assigns the men to sleep in Petit's study. Except for the hard, wooden floor and the heat and the smell of mold, I think this idea is fantastic. The space is still packed with old books and many glass cases containing artifacts, like wax seals that Vausse's prior used to validate his official letters. I make a comment to the effect that we should be careful not to set up too close to the glass cases, lest there be some unfortunate, glass shattering accident in the night.

I frequently lead study abroad programs with university students and as a professor I've grown accustomed to telling them what to do, as needed. This doesn't mean that they always do what I tell them, but they never question my authority or my right to make these requests. I'm also concerned, perhaps hyper-concerned, with the behavior of any group I travel with in a foreign country. I don't want to damage our hosts' stuff or offend them in any way and I especially want to avoid giving off that vibe of the "ugly American." I mention this by way of explaining that my comment, "be careful not to set up too close to the glass cases, lest there be some unfortunate, glass shattering accident in the night," didn't go over very well. Joe, one of the new pilgrims, takes offense right away. He doesn't like my assumption that he might be disrespectful of the space being offered to us, or that he would absent-mindedly leave his kit in such a manner that could cause damage to property.

Knowing myself and my own intentions, I think this is an overreaction. But Joe doesn't know me, or my intentions, or my own inflated sense of my role on this trip. Joe must simply think that I'm being an arse, and maybe I am. Saint Basil, where are you?

Please send some of that Christian charity my way. While I am occasionally an arse, I'm trending at about 90% of apologizing right away, as soon as I realize my error. Apologies don't instantly make hurt feelings go away, but you have to start somewhere. And it isn't as easy as "Joe will be gone in a week and that will be that." He's with us for two weeks, then leaves and come backs, then leaves and comes back again. He becomes a core member of the Pluscarden pilgrimage and I still see him from time to time.

This seems like a ridiculous little story, but it shows how difficult it can be when a silly offense becomes a first impression and each party struggles to let go and move on.

There's a great story from the writings of the desert fathers (or maybe I saw it on the 1970s TV show "Kung Fu"). Two monks are walking along the river when they see a woman who is struggling to cross. The monks are strictly forbidden from any contact with women, but one of them ignores this rule and helps the woman by carrying her to the other side. The second monk can't believe what he's just seen. The more he thinks about it, the more it troubles him. He's about to report the first monk to their superiors, but he decides to confront him instead.

"I'm very upset that you touched that woman today," the second monk says. "You know that this is against our rules."

"Are you still carrying that woman?" the first monks says. "I put her down hours ago."

This will be a good one for after-dinner story time.

14 June

We're in Fontenay, home of another famous Cistercian abbey. We divert from the pilgrimage to take a tour. I've been here a couple of times before, but Fontenay never fails to impress. Like Vausse and so many other monasteries, Fontenay suffered much damage and neglect during the French Revolution. The monks were forced to leave and, for a while, Fontenay operated as a paper mill. At the start of the 20th century, a banker from Lyon named

Edouard Aynard purchased the abbey and began restoring it. There are patiently executed historical reconstructions, educational features with good signage, and beautifully manicured gardens. Fontenay is now a UNESCO World Heritage Site.

Everything's going pear-shaped!

Tomasz is threatening to quit. Jai has lost his cool. Joe still runs hot and cold because of the patronizing tone I used with him. Chris snaps at me because his efforts to film the pilgrimage are getting no support. The Spaniel, young Andy, is in crisis and wants to leave the pilgrimage and go to Amsterdam for the weekend. He's tremendously immature and is starting to play up the fact that this whole pilgrimage thing was not his idea. Meanwhile, Father Giles's mother has died so he'll be gone for four days to attend her funeral. And David's wife is seriously ill. Not sure what's happening there, but it means that David will be less present on the pilgrimage.

Is this really only the second week? Oh, my God …

15 June

In Châtillon-sur-Seine, we stay at a convent of the Sisters of Charity. This is yet another religious guest house where the accommodations are simple but welcoming. To keep the place clean, the Sisters of Charity have a strict "No dogs!" rule. There's no place to camp close to where we're staying, so we have to figure out what to do with Rinnes, Al's yellow lab. Rinnes is well-behaved and has short, beige hair, so his impact on the guesthouse would be minimal. Father Giles and I create a diversion. Speaking to the mother superior of the house, who is also acting as the guest master, we direct her attention to some architectural feature of the building and ask for explanation. When she turns to look in this direction, Al and Rinnes sneak into the guest house behind her back. I'm ashamed to admit that our subterfuge fills me with boyish glee, but why? Why hoodwink a nun who's shown us nothing but hospitality and kindness? Perhaps some of my pilgrimage today will need to serve as an act of contrition.

I wake in the middle of the night thinking that the Spaniel has escaped to Amsterdam. Why do I care? He isn't my kid. He isn't my student. He's legally an adult. As it turns out, he's still here. Shows up for breakfast moody, but a little better than the day before.

Joe and I seem to be doing better, having some normal interactions without tension. Glad I apologized.

Meanwhile the rift between Tomasz and Jai is deepening. Tomasz says he's not going to drive today. I'm not sure how that's going to work. With David and Father Giles gone, I feel like I should step up and try to mediate, but maybe it's better if I stay out of it.

While Jai and Tomasz argue about whether Tomasz will drive the van, a bread truck rolls up and delivers a huge sack of baguette for the guesthouse. I buy myself a *pain au chocolat* from the driver. Oh, yes! *Très bon!* We're eating so well the pilgrims have begun joking that this is one of the few long-distance walks where people may actually gain weight. By the way, Tomasz does end up driving.

16-18 June

We've had three nights sleeping in parish halls, one in Bar-sur-Aube and two in Brienne-le-Château because it's the weekend. On all of these nights we've had family-style dinners around a big table (rather than everyone stooping with their camping bowl next to their sleeping bag). I bought a pocketknife in Brienne-le-Château, a Laguiole—the Cadillac of French knives—with an elegant, gently-curved, wooden handle made from old wine casks, a single four-inch blade, and a corkscrew. The knife comes in handy many times during the pilgrimage, but on that night, dining in the shadow of the Église Saint-Pierre-et-Saint-Paul, I show it off by opening all the bottles of wine.

Everyone takes turns sharing childhood memories. Some of the stories are funny, some are moving. They highlight the diversity in the group, but also our common humanity. The week-two pilgrims

Dinner behind the Église Saint-Pierre-et-Saint-Paul, Brienne-le-Château.

are gelling nicely with the rest of the group and it's sad to think that tomorrow some of them will be leaving.

On Saturday, I have a lovely walk with Maria of the open-toed sandals. Her brother, František, is visiting from the Czech Republic. He was an activist priest during the Prague Spring and was arrested for dissidence in 1968, when Soviet tanks rolled into the city. Before that happened, he sent Maria to London and told her not to come home. She was only eighteen at the time (remarkably, the same age as the Spaniel). She's lived in the UK ever since. We talk about growing up Catholic. Maria's brother doesn't speak English and I don't speak Czech, so Maria translates. I tell them the story of my confirmation, in which I had a crisis of faith at the last minute and walked out. Maria finds this very brave for a 13-year-old but assures me that if her own children had tried that she would have whacked them upside the head.

We're finally getting to the point, all of us, I think, where we can have deeper conversations. Traveling on foot, at a slower pace, helps make that possible. Maria and her brother move on and I'm left in the forest, completely at peace. I climb into a hunter's blind for a better view. Below me, I watch a fox sniff around the base of the blind, unaware of my presence, or more likely not caring.

3

Brienne-le-Château
to Laon

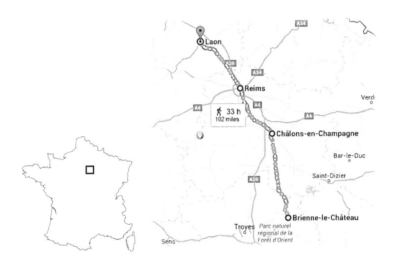

19 June

Three pilgrims from Elgin arrive: Tomas and Posie, a charming married couple, and Veronica, a wisp of a woman who's brought a very large and heavy suitcase that she somehow manages to haul up and down the steps of our lodgings, or wherever she needs to go, never once asking for help. Impressive. The three of them walk together and they prove themselves to be determined hikers, even on the hottest of days.

The situation between Tomasz and Jai is getting worse. Jai can feel overbearing and he adopts a military posture in most interactions. But there's something much more serious happening with Tomasz that goes beyond personality clashes. He chain-smokes and drinks a dozen or more beers every night. He no longer eats with the group but sustains himself with pre-cooked sausages. Some of the pilgrims have spoken openly about how they hope the pilgrimage will be transformative, bringing positive changes to their lives. This might happen for Tomasz, whatever's going on with him, but the pressures of driving and the other staff duties are taking a toll. I and others reach out, but to no avail. I feel for him.

Robbie is another puzzle for me. I'm guessing we're about the same age. He's a retired lawyer, very fit from golfing all the time, and walking. He actually helped reconnoitered some of the routes in France before the pilgrimage commenced. He's very smart and witty and, I think, accustomed to being in charge. Sometimes I really like him and other times we clash—two alpha males.

The rash on my bum is still there. (This is not connected to Robbie, I just couldn't think of a good segue.) I've moved away from the spider bite diagnosis and am now thinking shingles. I really don't want to go to the doctor and, unfortunately, there's no one here that I feel comfortable enough asking for help.

"Excuse me, _____. Would you mind looking at this thing on my bum?" No. That won't do.

We take a nice swim in the River Aube today. Chris shoots some footage of kids jumping their bikes off a ramp and into the river. As much as we're doing our "pilgrimage thing," we still encounter much of normal daily life.

A new crop of pilgrims arrives. This includes three of Iain's brothers, Andrew, Michael, and Gregory, all of whom also play bagpipes. Now that some guys his age are here, Andy (the Spaniel) has decided to stay. It's fun to watch him play the "expert pilgrim" with them. I can't imagine how bored he must have been hanging out with so many people his parents' age and older. The core group is getting better at orienting the newcomers to our ways: the claiming of sleeping space, the copying of maps, etc. Well oriented, with neatly-drawn maps and plenty of water in our day packs, the walk takes us through large open fields cultivated with grains. There aren't many trees so it feels hot without the shade, but we all make it without incident to Le-Meix-Tiercelin.

Our accommodations for tonight are a psychiatric hospital.

I'm still trying to figure out if David simply has really good connections or if desperation is the reason for some of the places we're staying. It could not have been easy finding rooms for so many people in many of the villages where we sleep. And the expense of staying in hotels or B&Bs would have been prohibitive. One aspect of our travel that defines it as a real pilgrimage is our dependence on the kindness of strangers. All the parish halls and monasteries we've encountered thus far have donated whatever space they had to offer. Remember, the pilgrimage is meant as a fundraiser for Pluscarden's building project, so managing costs is important. Acknowledging all of this, let me just repeat that earlier sentence:

Our accommodations for tonight are a psychiatric hospital.

This is humbling, but also jarring, when we consider that just days ago we were in a 13th-century monastery being used as a movie set. Every day is a new adventure.

The scene in the psychiatric hospital is really quite calm. Lots of clients who seem heavily sedated wander the grounds. Rosnay l'Hopital is actually a farm on which all of the clients work, growing and selling flowers and vegetables as part of their treatment. Our sleeping arrangement is in a big open space on a top floor of the hospital. Again, find the floor space that will offer you the best night's sleep.

The food at Rosnay is very good, especially for an institutional cafeteria. The pilgrims arrive first and stand at the head of the queue, but when the patients arrive, everyone in our group makes way so that the clients can go first. This is a very Christian gesture, unfortunately it reinforces a separation between our two groups, the so-called "sick" and the so-called "well." I stay where I am and it leads to some interesting conversations with the regular residents.

The weather is pleasant and we take our trays outside to eat at picnic tables in an open courtyard. The residents are seated all around us and it definitely feels like they're observing us as much as we're observing them. At one point, Chris goes back inside to refill his coffee, leaving a large piece of cake on the table. Al looks around and reaches over with his spoon to take a bite. Someone else follows, then someone else, then me. As this happens, the residents around us watch and giggle at Chris's response when he returns to find his cake mostly eaten. His over-dramatic reaction does not disappoint. It's a wonderful shared moment.

20 June

Today we head for Mairy-sur-Marne.

The confluence of conversations around the breakfast table is wonderful. There's a backgammon lesson taking place on a smart phone. Chris is trying to teach Jai how to put Excel on his iPad. Robbie and Al are organizing the maps. People are talking about the weather and how they slept and what they hope we're having for dinner.

"This isn't so much a pilgrimage as a walking holiday," Robbie proclaims. "A real pilgrimage should be continuous." He's not totally wrong. There follows some debate on this question, but for once I don't participate. I just listen. I remember that that's the first word in the *Rule of Saint Benedict*: "Listen." As the debate continues, I realize that the pilgrimage isn't the route or the destination or whether we do it continuously or in bits and bobs.

The pilgrimage is the people.

Today, the pilgrims' stamina and resolve are put to the test. The path they're on is an ancient Roman road, paved stones in a straight line with nary a shade tree in sight. This is exactly what the Romans needed to quickly dispatch their legions throughout the empire. For pilgrims, it means boring scenery, a surface that's hard on the feet, with little to no protection from the sun.

This day also turns out to be the hottest day of the entire journey. Jai keeps busy driving up and down the path delivering extra water. I work with the support team that day and I'm thankful for the air-conditioned hall where we'll be sleeping that night. By the time they arrive at the parish hall in Mairy-sur-Marne, the pilgrims are spent, both physically and psychologically.

Pilgrims take refuge from the heat: l-r, Richard, Maria, Tomas, Veronica, and Posie.

The villagers at Mairy-sur-Marne are genuinely excited to welcome the pilgrims to their parish hall. They've set an elegant table and are bringing wine and food at 7. At 5, parishioners will pick up small groups of pilgrims and take them to their homes for showers or baths.

Robbie and Julia, a new pilgrim from Germany, are among the first to arrive. Robbie immediately does what any self-respecting pilgrim does upon arrival, sets up his sleeping space. He decides that, of all the spots in the hall, the best space for him is beside the elegant dining table the parishioners have laid out. He starts rearranging things to his liking. I intervene.

"Hey, Robbie," I say. "Would it be possible to wait to get settled till after dinner. The townsfolk have set this nice table and they'll be joining us later for dinner. We might try to keep it nice for them."

I'm probably making myself sound much kinder and more reasonable than I actually was. All I remember is Robbie's response.

"I'll set up when and wherever I bloody well please!" says Robbie. Then comes Julia's response.

"Leave my friend alone!"

Unexpected, I thought. They seem to have no sense of anything except themselves. I'm trying to look out for them and maintain relationships with the locals. I leave the hall in a huff and go outside where steam is coming off the pavement in waves. It never occurs to me that Robbie and Julia's responses are directly related to the heat, which they've been walking in all day. I've been driving in the air-conditioned van or setting up in the air-conditioned hall. Al comes out and calmly explains this to me. I'm sensing that he'll be my rock on this trip. Whether it's his leadership experience in the RAF or raising two daughters, he's got a cool head and reads people very well. He reads Julia's mini-meltdown as too much heat exposure.

"Some of these blokes have been pushed beyond their physical limits," he says. "Don't take it personally."

Shortly thereafter, the shower convoy arrives. A sturdy French woman named Mme. Bonhomme is in charge. Imagine the intensity of Eisenhower planning the invasion at Normandy, then multiply times seven, and you have Mme. Bonhomme. She has a list of every parishioner who is going to drive pilgrims to their homes to freshen up, and how many pilgrims each parishioner will take. Mme. Bonhomme and the parishioners speak no English. None of the pilgrims, except me, speaks French. Here's the gist of the conversation.

"Thank you so much," I say in French. "Thank you all for opening your homes to us. These showers will be especially welcome on such a hot day."

"But, of course. Of course," says Mme. Bonhomme in French. "Now, to the list. Marie-Claire, you can take two, *oui?*"

Marie-Claire steps forward and replies, "*Oui.*" Mme. Bonhomme turns to me, holds up her thumb and forefinger and says, "*Deux.*"

I turn to the pilgrims and say that two people can go in the first car, though this must be obvious with both Mme. Bonhomme and myself holding up two digits. Husband and wife Tomas and Posie cautiously volunteer for the first car. Mme. Bonhomme returns to her list.

"Jacqueline. You can take two."

"*Oui.*"

Digits once again flash like gang signs in south central Los Angeles.

"Two," I say, and two more pilgrims depart with their generous host. This repeats several times until, with half the pilgrims still unassigned, Mme. Bonhomme gets to Monique.

"Monique. You can take two?"

"I can take four," Monique announces.

"*Non,*" says Mme. Bonhomme. "The list says you can take two."

"But I can take four," Monique says as she gestures toward the remaining hot and sweaty bodies still waiting for transport to a shower.

"Don't try to show off," says Mme. Bonhomme. "Other ladies have signed up, too, and you can't just take them all!"

"I'm not showing off. I'm trying to be helpful."

And so on, for what seems like five minutes. There is no way to jump into their conversation and no use translating for the English speakers, who are growing more and more impatient. Finally, Monique acquiesces and takes two pilgrims. We get through the rest of Mme. Bonhomme's list, the pilgrims depart, and calm returns to the parish hall. I don't assign myself to a shower. I've been in air-conditioning since morning so I don't really need a shower, but the rule is never to pass up a shower, since you don't know whether you'll get one tomorrow. No matter, I think. The peace and quiet of the hall will be rejuvenating enough.

I go to the *boulangerie* to get baguettes for dinner and for the next day's lunches. The group plans a 5:30 am departure, to beat the heat. The *boulangerie* won't be open that early, hence the need to shop the evening before. The bakery has extravagant fruit tartelettes, so I buy one each for Robbie and Julia as a peace offering.

Posie and Tomas are the first to return from their baths. "Not showers," Posie says. "Baths!" Each of them is holding a bottle of Champagne, a gift from their hosts. "It's real *champagne*," Tomas points out in his best French accent, "because we've entered the Champagne territory." Al is the next one back, with his own stories of steaming hot showers and conversations with his hosts in *Franglais*.

To his credit, when Robbie returns he immediately comes to me and asks, "Are we okay?" In spite of my earlier read on him, he does have some awareness.

A lovely drink with the parishioners of Mairy-sur-Marne, with many speeches welcoming us to their town. It's fun to see people trying to piece together sentences in languages they barely know. There's a sincerity in their effort that's charming. The locals depart, leaving us an amazing home-cooked meal, much of it prepared with produce from their own farms or gardens. After dinner, there is much joy over the return of Father Giles from his mother's funeral.

I feel "outside" the group. I wonder if others feel the same. I know that I'm integral to the project, but I feel unappreciated. Blah-blah-blah. I can't be the only one feeling this way. It was fun to be able to translate today, but even that sets me off as "special." It must feel to the others like I'm managing the information they receive, but this is really just a product of how slowly my brain works. Maria tells me this afternoon that she appreciates the way I'm trying to be sensitive to our hosts. It feels good to hear that. Then a question occurs to me. What if I'm called to make this pilgrimage happen for others and not for myself? What if *my* pilgrimage is to help them have *their* pilgrimage?

21 June

We spend the evening in a parish hall in Ambonnay. A lovely young family lives in the adjacent house and manages the space. The wife runs a pre-school out of one of the rooms, which is filled with small furniture. The children, Malot (9) and Faustine (4) are charmers. Malot has somehow taught himself to juggle so we juggle together to the delight of our audience of parents and pilgrims. Pete cooks hotdogs and hamburgers on the now fully-functioning cooker. It's a regular *fête américaine*.

22 June

Today, the walk ends at the cathedral of Reims. I give two presentations to groups of pilgrims arriving at staggered times. Robbie makes a point of telling me, in front of the group, that he won't be attending either talk, since he's already seen the Reims cathedral—subtext: "there's nothing I can possibly learn from you, professor." Whatever.

Both of the talks go well. In fact, I'm rather brilliant, considering I've forgotten most of what I learned in my undergrad art history courses and need to refresh my memory by reading the guidebook two hours earlier. Reims is an important stop, of course, because it's where Clovis was baptized as the first Frankish king to convert to Christianity, and from 1179 to 1825, it's where the French kings were crowned. During the Hundred Years War, Joan of Arc even won Reims back from the English so that Charles VII could hold his coronation in the cathedral. It's also one of the few medieval structures where we know the names of its architects: Jean d'Orbais, Jean le Loup, Gaucher de Reims, and Bernard de Soissons.

Father Giles celebrates Mass in the Marc Chagall chapel, one of several small chapels in the cathedral's apse. The chapel's windows were designed by the 20th-century artist. Chagall happened to be

Jewish, but his work here transcends divisions between faiths or denominations.

During today's walk, one of the women discovers that she's forgotten to pack any feminine hygiene products and finds herself in need on an isolated trail and nowhere near a pharmacy. She calls Jai who passes her request to Chris.

"Take the van and find a town where you can buy tampons," Jai says.

"What …"

Chris does not speak French and, according to his report, there is a good deal of miming and gesturing and awkward phrasing before realizing that the French word for "tampon" is … "tampon."

The day ends at the Benedictine abbey of Saint-Thiery. Once again, the monastic food and lodgings are excellent. This is the monastery where the 12th-century theologian and mystic William of Saint-Thiery served as abbot. After dinner, I tell the story of another mystic, the 14th-century pilgrim, Margery Kempe.

Margery is known to us through the story of her life, dictated to a monk, which some consider the first autobiography in English. After bearing her husband John some fourteen children, Margery had a vision in which Jesus instructed her to be celibate. She wasn't educated, but she was very devout. In the course of her life, she undertook many pilgrimages throughout Europe and the Holy Land. She was given the "gift of tears," which caused her to weep incessantly on account of Jesus's love for her and for all of humankind. This was a beautiful thing, unless Margery was part of your pilgrimage, in which case it became extremely annoying. Margery was actually abandoned several times by her fellow pilgrims when they could no longer stand her weeping.

Julia is experiencing some undefined conflict with Jai. In such close quarters, it's nearly impossible for others not to notice tensions between their fellow pilgrims. Robbie seems to be a comfort to her. They've paired off as walking partners and Julia seems grateful for Robbie's advice.

But tonight, Margery's story has an impact on Julia, who begins to sob quietly during the telling. She informs me later that she sees herself as Margery, feels that no one in the group likes her, and fears that we might abandon her.

"Oh, no," I say, commiserating. "That's not at all why I told the story."

Clearly the pilgrims continue to see themselves in these tales and some of them think that they contain messages and meanings that they must discern. I'll need to be more careful.

23 June

We're staying at a château above the town of Corbeny, near the Cistercian abbey of Clairvaux. I say that we're staying at the château, but we're really staying in rooms above a carriage house down the road from the château. The owners are two elegant aristocrats, a brother and sister, who have generously invited us up to their digs for champagne and hors d-oeuvres. The three brothers who are pipers play and march, as we marvel at the grand view of the town below.

After the bagpipes and champagne, I offer a story. Because our two hosts only speak French, I narrate in English for the pilgrims and Father Giles translates into French for our hosts. This has a great comic effect. I tell the "Pardoner's Tale," from Chaucer. It's the story of three companions being lured by the devil to a hidden cache of gold, and how the companions slowly kill each other off because each one is worried that the others will kill him first and take all the gold. The devil takes great joy in watching this happen. The pardoner's moral is repeated throughout the telling: *Cupiditas radix malorum est* (the love of money is the route of all evil).

Because we have three sibling bagpipers among us, I recast the story to be about them. The château becomes the site of the hidden cache of gold, which pleases our hosts. Robbie makes it clear that he's not interested in the story and leaves as soon as I begin. In Robbie's absence, I describe the devil so that everyone knows I mean him. Chaucer's version is great on its own, and my reframing is pretty good. But the star of the evening is Father Giles and his simultaneous translation, with which he takes many liberties. For example, whenever one of the greedy bagpiping brothers gets killed, he doesn't translate, but simply draws his thumb across his throat and makes that sound that pirates make when they're threatening to kill you.

24 June

Father Giles celebrates Mass at the ruins of Vauclair, Bouconville.

We have Mass this morning outside, at the ruins of Vauclair, a 12th-century monastery founded by the famous Cistercian monk, Bernard of Clairvaux. The air is crisp and the sun peaks over the trees just as Father Giles is elevating the Host and reciting the liturgy. "The body of Christ." Good timing, God.

We end our walk in the medieval city of Laon and I give a tour of its cathedral. My favorite story is of the sixteen, life-size statues of oxen that stand in the upper arcades of the west towers.

According to legend, the builders were struggling to raise stones to the upper levels, even with pulleys. Oxen miraculously appeared and helped with this task. The statues commemorate the oxen's part in building the cathedral.

The group dynamic is improving. Even Jai and Tomasz are talking to each other. We're staying in the small town of Liesse-Notre-Dame, east of Laon. There's a wedding happening and the bagpipers get themselves invited with an offering of music, which the wedding guests much appreciate. They suggest the rest of us can tag along, but only if we stay on the periphery. The bride's mother requests the song that's played "when the American firemen are buried," by which she means "Amazing Grace." Upon hearing it, she is moved to tears. Her grandmother was Scottish, and she has always heard the song on TV, never live. Many jigs follow. People dance and laugh.

Sadly, this is also an opportunity for Andy to show his inexperience in social settings and for Tomasz, too much in his cups, to act out. They seem unaware that only the pipers were invited, and not the pilgrims, who for the most part stand around the margins with every intention to leave before we wear out our welcome. Andy and Tomasz insert themselves between the pipers and the wedding couple, taking photos of both with no sense of how they might be disrupting a private event. Tomasz tries several times to dance with the bride and take pictures with her. The two of them are both offended when I encourage them to leave with the rest of us. Embarrassing for the two of them, and I imagine for Olga, who is remarkably calm and patient during all of Tomasz's troubles.

Laon *to*
Thérouanne

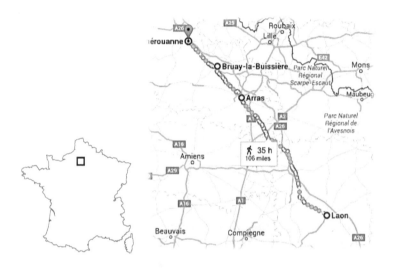

25 June

Sunday departures: Joe, Robbie, and Julia, bagpipers Andrew, Michael, and Gregory, Posie and Tomas, Veronica, and young Andy. What will happen to him? To all of them? How has the pilgrimage affected them and what will it mean to them later in life?

26 June

Driving out of Liesse-Notre-Dame to the drop-off point, we're stopped on the road by the butcher who owns the shop around the corner from our lodgings. We'd come too late to get anything on Saturday—we saw the butcher inside behind the locked door. The *boucherie* is closed on Sundays. Now, Monday morning, the butcher stops our van in the middle of the street and hands us pounds of sausages through the rolled down window. No charge. Just another act of kindness among many we encounter along the way.

27 June

Somewhere near Fontaine-lès-Clercs, Maria and I spot a large group of hikers on the horizon. I venture that they might be pilgrims and we try to guess where they could be headed. Maria suggests that there's no way they're traveling as far as we are.

"I mean, we're walking all the way from Burgundy to the north of Scotland!" she says. It turns out they are pilgrims, with a program very similar to what we're doing: a small group of about nine traveling the entire route, with a support staff, and other pilgrims joining a week at a time along the way. And they are walking slightly further than we are: from London to Jerusalem to raise awareness of the Israeli-Palestinian conflict. Maria and I both feel smaller when we learn this and laugh at our own arrogance.

28 June

It's the middle of week 4. Only the eight regular pilgrims are here, the "family," as we now refer to ourselves: Al, Maria, Chris, Jai, Pete, Father Giles, Rinnes the lab, and me.

We move from Liesse-Notre-Dame so quickly that I can't remember where we are on Monday night (some parish hall in Tergnier). Tuesday, we stay in a guest house in Vermand, run by the Poor Clares, the women's branch of the Franciscans.

Tonight, we're in an agricultural training school, staying in the dorms because the school is out of session. Pete takes the day off to walk with the pilgrims. He still has a lot of work to do, even though he won't be cooking tonight, but I think he enjoys (and needs) the break.

Being in a different place every night there's a real risk that this whole adventure will become a blur. We're on a schedule, which means we rarely have time to stay in one place and get to know it.

We have a great discussion tonight about how to decide who should get a private room or comfy bed when these limited resources become available. Should this be decided based upon age? Physical need? Gender? So far the men have been chivalrous and the (liberated) women have accepted this chivalry, preferring the comfy sleeping quarters to any tedious protests over equal treatment. It's quite an interesting talk with every participant revealing something about themselves.

"Since we're on a pilgrimage," I ask, "what would Jesus do?"

Al also introduces the pilgrims to the drinking game "ibble-dibble," a mixture of tongue-twister and memory game combined with too much drinking. Hilarious!

We've all started playing games in our downtime. Maria has a travel edition of Scrabble, where the tiles stick to the board. I've taught Chris and Pete to play Mill, a.k.a., Nine Men's Morris, an ancient strategy game that was known to the Romans. It's a great game for travel because you don't need to carry anything. You can create the "board" by drawing in the dirt, then all you need are some stones or coins to act as markers. For a few weeks, we become obsessed with the game, then let it drop and only play occasionally.

29 June

We're in the medieval town of Arras and I've decided to take a day for myself. I check into the downtown Hotel Ibis midmorning and immediately take a long hot bath before I tour the city.

Arras lies midway between Paris and Calais, south of the River Scarpe. Settlement here dates back to the Gallic Iron Age, long before Julius Caesar ever wrote that "All Gaul is divided into three parts, one of which the Belgae inhabit." Those ancient Belgians account for some of the town's distinct cultural flavor. Arras was a frontier town—French, but with a strong Belgian influence. Indeed, one of the lasting impressions from a visit to Arras is the opulent Flemish facades on the Grand Place. The first, high stone house in the Grand Place was constructed in the 12th century.

The Place des Héros, Arras.

A short walk from the Grand Place is the Place des Héros, named in honor of the 240 suspected members of the French Resistance whom the Nazis executed there. The centerpiece of the Place des Héros is the Hôtel de Ville, the old town hall, with its soaring belfry tower that beckons visitors from afar into the city. It takes me about twenty minutes to climb the tower's winding staircase to the top—the giant clock's ticking growing louder the higher up I go. On arrival at the top, I'm treated to spectacular views: rolling hills in the distance, neatly ordered Dutch-style houses surrounding the town, and just below, shops and cafes and food trucks around the square with something for every taste. On this particular day, the local pop station, RadioActive, is doing a live broadcast. The music ranges from Zamfir on the pan pipes to rap to Johnny Cash.

I'm having all sort of memories of busking in big public plazas like this. (I was a clown in an earlier life.) I imagine watching the medieval vernacular plays that I've only read about in books being performed here, with titles like *The Courtly Lad of Arras*, *The Boy and the Blind Man*, and *The Play about Robin and Marion*. Arras was also the centre of a group of poets called the *trouvères*, who wrote songs of courtly love. One of these, Moniot of Arras, wrote the 13th-century hit, *Ce fut en mai (It happened in May)*, about a man who follows two lovers into a garden seeking solace for his own unrequited love. Here's a taste of the lyrics in medieval French, the *langue d'oi*, with a translation in English:

Ce fut en mai	It happened in May,
Au douz tens gai	when skies are gay
Que la saisons est bele,	how beautiful the season,
Main me levai,	At break of day
Joer m'alai	I rose to play
Lez une fontenele.	Beside a little fountain.

Such performances seem like ghosts now, that you won't even see in your imagination unless you know that they once dominated the cultural life of Arras. Now the 1950s band leader Louis Prima belts out "Just a gigolo" through Radio Active's loudspeakers and my medieval reverie is gone.

During World War I, German artillery destroyed the Hôtel de Ville and the buildings around it. All of them were rebuilt after the war to try to recapture their original, medieval character. The two wars are also ever-present in our experiences here. Hiking through grain fields and forests, some of our pilgrims encounter unexploded ordinance from World War I. Young Andy decides to take a petrified hand grenade as a souvenir. The thought that it might still explode is frightening and the Spaniel is finally convinced to turn the grenade into the local police.

I sit all afternoon in an outdoor café under one of the colonnades, drinking *thé au lait*, which the waiter calls *thé Espagnol*.

Yuck-yuck. Get it? *Au lait. Olé*! Later, with dinner, I have to try a blond beer with a label called Abbaye de Vaucelle, though I don't think it's brewed by monks anymore. I sleep well in my soft hotel bed. My poor fellow pilgrims sleep on the floor of a church hall.

Next morning, I return to the group without an ounce of guilt for having taken a self-care day. Is this a "real" pilgrimage? I don't know anymore. Surely medieval pilgrims must have had their own versions of taking a time out from the group for some much-needed alone time. To be honest, in this moment, I don't really care about the question of "what is a pilgrimage?"

Back among the pilgrims, Tomasz continues his downward spiral. The tension between Jai's desire for the pilgrimage to run with military precision and Father Giles's Christian take on the shepherd not abandoning his sheep is coming to a head. Olga returns to Scotland tomorrow. What will anchor Tomasz to the group when she's gone?

30 June

A parish hall in the village of Houdain. A generally good vibe among the pilgrims. It's only 8pm but people are heading to bed. There is a round of "good nights" that reminds me of the TV show *The Waltons*, where every member of the large, close-knit family says goodnight to every other member, every night.

1 July

I walk with Al, Pete, and Maria today, from Houdain to Thérouanne. It starts out rainy, but the weather turns cool and sunny after lunch. Al sticks with us until lunch is over, then his long legs and fit body call him to move at his faster pace. Maria and I are getting better at reading the maps, so we introduce Pete to the idea of incorporating shortcuts that bring us to the RV point sooner. We end our hike by dipping our tired feet into an icy cold stream. Perfect.

We stay the night at a pilgrims' retreat that resembles a modern youth hostel more than anything else. Al is already there and he's started prepping for dinner so that Pete can have another night off from cooking. I join him right away, since we each have our own real beds and there's no reason for the usual scrambling upon arrival.

Just after dinner, we're all invited to Thérouanne's History Centre. The mayor of Thérouanne presents Father Giles with a stone from the town's cathedral, destroyed in 1553 by Charles V, to be used in construction of the new building at Pluscarden.

Several French media outlets are present. They interview Father Giles and me about the pilgrimage and its purpose. A lovely young *journaliste* asks me, "Is this a *real* pilgrimage?"

I smile.

5

Thérouanne *to* Calais
to Dover *to* London

2 July

I walk to the top of the hill in Thérouanne to see the ruins of the cathedral. Nothing there but a nice public park with a lovely view.

There's a large map on the wall of the pilgrim's retreat labeled "*le Monde.*" It's stuck with pins, each one representing the origin point of a pilgrim who's stayed there. Lots of pins from the UK and Europe. One each from South Africa, New Zealand, and China. I stick one in at Minnesota. Maria spends several minutes studying the map and pondering the range of visitors who have stayed there. Mass is held in the local church, just across the street. Father Giles celebrates in French. This is one of the better attended services because local folk are there, in addition to our smaller pilgrim group. Mass is such an important service that the monks offer to the pilgrimage. I find myself disappointed on their behalf when pilgrims don't come. Today, the church's nave is almost full, but I have to remind myself that there is something bigger going on, beyond the numbers. The words from Matthew's Gospel come to mind: "where two or three are gathered in My name, there am I among them."

Two new pilgrims join us this week: Lena, a retired elementary school teacher, and Eric, another retired soldier, both Scottish. I beat Chris in a game of Mill, then teach Pete to play and lose. This triggers a memory from the fourth grade when I taught my then best friend to play chess and he beat me in our first game, and every game since. He then stopped being my best friend, though I don't think that was connected to chess.

Tomasz spends the day cleaning out the van that we borrowed from la Pierre-qui-Vire. A couple of their monks will rendezvous with us tomorrow. Tomasz continues to be anti-social (staying to himself, not eating with the group), but at least he's not actively causing problems, as he sometimes has.

3 July

Another long day. We depart Thérouanne for Alquines. I walk with Maria most of the way. The route is largely forest interspersed with small towns and villages.

Arcane architectural history alert:

There's an interesting church in Cléty dedicated to Saint Léger. Its foundation date is uncertain, but the dedication of the bell tower dates to the 1650s.

The church of Saint Omer in Remilly-Wirquin was built to accommodate the village's small population (roughly 300). It's a cozy church with simple, white-washed interior walls, not big enough to have side aisles or clerestory windows. A small section is said to date from the thirteenth century, but there's been a lot of reconstruction. The church's adjacent cemetery is entirely covered in gravel, but there is indeed a working water spigot and my confirming this makes Maria happy.

We stop for lunch at the church of Saint Pétronille in Acuin-Westbécourt. This must have been a lovely country church when it was first constructed in the 12ᵗʰ century. The architectural historian Pierre Héliot described it in his monumental work, *Les églises du Moyen-âge dans le Pas-de-Calais* (Medieval Churches in the Pas-de-Calais). According to Héliot, the church was "*malheureusement restaurée avec indiscrétion au XIXᵉ siècle*" (sadly restored with indiscretion in the 19ᵗʰ century). You can say that again.

Over lunch, I tell Maria what little I know from the life of Pétronille—the church's namesake—which is one of the more frustrating saints' lives I've read. Pétronille (Petronilla, in Latin), was first thought to be the daughter of Saint Peter, but this was probably because their names were so similar. Later writers called her Peter's "spiritual daughter," his acolyte. Peter cured Pétronille of palsy, but later, when he felt she was faltering in her spiritual progress, he asked God to strike Pétronille with a fever, from which Peter wouldn't cure her until she returned to living righteously. Another story tells of Peter locking Pétronille in a tower because he found her too beautiful and wanted to keep men at a distance—shades of Rapunzel. Suitors came anyway, but Pétronille refused their advances. She died in the tower of a hunger strike. Sad, and weird.

We end the day's walk at the church of Saint-Nicolas d'Alquines, a 16ᵗʰ-century construction whose tower makes it the tallest building in the village, thus an ideal choice for the final pick-up because it's easy to find.

Waiting for our ride, I begin to ponder. Will doing this pilgrimage for thirteen weeks be any different than doing it for five weeks? Will it just be more beautiful countryside, more charming churches in charming villages, more tension within the group that turns to playfulness that turns to love and respect and then back into tension? What will be different as things progress? Pilgrim's progress?

Staying in the abbey of Wisque tonight. Dinner in the refectory. The abbot pours water over our hands to wash them as we enter. We eat in silence. The *Rule of Benedict* is read in Latin, followed by a biography of Pope John-Paul II read in French. Copying maps after dinner tonight, Maria teases Al about his fascination with maps.

"You look at maps and see mileage," Al says. "I look at them and see a stream, a small village, a forest with many interesting sites."

A big admin meeting after dinner tonight. Packing and repacking the vans. I'm anxious.

Tomorrow we cross the channel for England. There's a stillness in the group. Could it be connected to this big transition? Or am I just imagining things? Traveling in the UK will certainly be easier in many ways. More familiar territory. No language issues. That last one will make the shopping much easier for Pete. His French has actually improved over five weeks and I'm proud of him, if I may say so, for not giving up. But Pete's also leaving us after we get to the UK, and new cooks will be coming on board.

Big transitions. We'll see ...

4 July

England.

The ferry ride from Calais to Dover is uneventful, though I have some trouble getting through passport control. All sorts of questions about where I've been and the stamps in my passport. I tend to think the border officers are having a bit of fun with the Yank, since this is the period when Donald Trump first starts wreaking so much havoc with foreigners coming into the US.

Happy Fourth of July.

David meets us at a petrol station near the port at Dover. He greets me with a hug and a big smile.

"My brother," he says.

Tonight, we stay in the convent of Minster Abbey in Kent. Father Giles is in the "priest's room," which has its own shower. The men are sharing a common room called "Saint Benedict's," but many, including myself, are taking advantage of the fair weather and sleeping outside, within the monastery's walls.

Minster Abbey, Kent.

Alice Warrender has just arrived. She's one of the patrons of the Pluscarden 1230 Pilgrimage. I suppose that means she lends her name to give the pilgrimage some gravitas. Alice was in a terrible bicycle accident and undertook a pilgrimage from Canterbury to Rome as part of her healing process. She wrote a book about it, *An Accidental Jubilee*, so she's now something of a celebrity pilgrim.

Some in the group have read her book and some are in the middle of reading it. Everyone is quite interested to find out what she's like. When we finally meet, my first impression is of a warm and kind person, though I'm told there are moments in her book when she doesn't come off that way. She's beautiful, in that youthful, let-me-flip-my-luxurious-hair-out-of-my-face kind of way. I like her.

The drone is up, taking shots for the documentary. It's annoying buzz provides contrast to the serene monastic setting. I've taken a liking to Chris, even though he's a spacey 25-year-old. I think he appreciates that I take him seriously as an artist, which I think he is.

Vespers takes place in Latin, outside in the convent's garden and the nuns invite us to join in. Afterwards, we have dinner in the garden as well. Maria and I chat with Sister Benedict, who tells an amazing story of her cancer being cured by the relic of Saint Mildred, one of the founders of Minster Abbey back in the late 7th century. Maria tells us that her brother, the priest, was also miraculously cured of cancer by praying to Saint John Ogilvie, a Scottish priest who was martyred after the Reformation. I find it odd for a Czech priest to pray to a Scottish saint, but since both the saint and Maria's brother were persecuted priests, it makes more sense. Interesting that my mind goes to which saint the brother should pray to for a cancer cure, and not whether saints can cure cancer at all.

The calm of the evening and the joy of the nuns remind me of our time at Val-Saint-Benoît. My reflex is to speak French to the Minster Abbey nuns. Al jokes that he'd be happy to act as translator now, since he's not sure if the locals will understand "American."

The hour of Compline is chanted in English. The same Psalms are chanted at this hour in every Benedictine monastery, according to Saint Benedict's *Rule*: Psalms 4, 90 and 133. Here's the last line from Psalm 4 (the NIV translation), so you can see why it's such a good choice for the end of the day:

In peace, I will lie down and sleep,
    for you alone, LORD,
    make me dwell in safety.

Watching dusk turn to darkness, I fall asleep under the stars. Most of the guys are dispersed throughout the garden. In the distance, a train rolls across its tracks. Doves coo overhead. From the guest house, I hear faint women's voices.

5 July

We walk to Canterbury today. Of course, what else should pop into my head but the famous lines from Chaucer's General Prologue, which every student of the *Canterbury Tales* is forced to memorize.

And specially, from every shires ende
Of Engelond, to Caunterbury they wende,
The hooly blisful martir for to seke,
That hem hath holpen whan that they were seeke.

To seek the holy, blissful martyr, who helped them when they were sick. For the sake of my fellow Yanks, who may not know the story, the "hooly blisful martir" is Thomas Becket, who was slain in Canterbury Cathedral in 1170 by two thugs of King Henry II, with whom Becket was having a theological disagreement over who had the right to try clergymen accused of serious crimes. Henry said it was the king. Becket sided with the church. When Henry had had enough of the uppity archbishop, he asked (rhetorically), "Who will rid me of this meddlesome priest?" Two of his knights answered the question by murdering Becket as he prayed at the altar. You can see the spot where it happened when you go inside the church. Medieval society declared Becket an instant martyr and pilgrimages to the site of his murder have been happening ever since.

Outside the cathedral, a buoyant woman whom I don't know approaches me.

"Are you the professor?" she asks in a heavy Scottish brogue.

"I am *a* professor," I say.

"No. You're *the* professor. From the pilgrimage. From Pluscarden." It's Ann, one of our new cooks, who has seen my picture on Pluscarden's website.

"In that case, yes," I say. "I *am* the professor."

We sit on a bench inside Canterbury's gates and wait for the other pilgrims to arrive. Once they do, David has arranged a tour.

One of the traditions at Canterbury is to crawl up a set of steps on one's knees to reach the Becket sanctuary, which all of the pilgrims in our group attempt. It's hard on my knees, and I give out just three steps from the top. So much for experimental archeology. Then I watch Ann, who has just joined the group an hour before. She doesn't hesitate before she gets down on her knees and slowly, painfully, crawls up the stone steps, one by one. She's incredibly brave, and it looks excruciating. She needs help on the final step and Father Giles comes to her aid.

Well done, Ann.

Chapter 28 of the *Rule of Benedict* concerns a "brother who refuses correction." This seems to be where Tomasz's story is headed. After talking and negotiating and praying to help Tomasz, the final solution Benedict offers when the brother "is not healed even in this way" is to let the abbot "use the knife of amputation." David is hardly the abbot, but he is the pilgrimage director and takes his responsibility to the group seriously. He decides to send Tomasz home at the end of the week. Tomasz is obviously upset. Sending him home was the plan I had advocated for, but now I feel guilty. Tomasz has admitted to being clinically depressed and having trouble with alcohol. Those are powerful demons, and it's unreasonable for me or anyone else to expect his behavior to magically change just because we ask him to. He needs help and I'm not sure the pilgrimage is the right kind.

Then it occurs to me that maybe Tomasz was sent here to help *us*: to become more patient? to learn more empathy? to see Christ in others? If that's the case, it feels like the pilgrimage has failed, or at least I have.

6 July

After the hottest of showers, I sleep in the softest bed I've ever experienced: crisp white sheets, goose feather duvet. I share the bed with David, which is a bit comical, but it works out fine. I'll just confirm that this is a large bed and each of us has plenty of room on our respective sides. Good news today from David's wife. Her condition has improved and the specialists seem hopeful. All of this happens in the country home of Amanda Cottrell, whom the writer Harry Bucknall has dubbed the "Queen of Kent," on account of her hospitality and magnanimity. She cooks us a fabulous meal and is gracious and charming throughout our stay.

We walk along the coast from Canterbury to Faversham today. A cool 36° C (97 ° F). No shade. I meet the warden of a bird sanctuary on the way, as she counts terns while nude sunbathing. (It's a very isolated walk, so I think we were both surprised.) Some very good conversation once the awkwardness passes.

Some of my walk today is with Alice, our celebrity pilgrim. We talk about trying to figure life out, her happy marriage and how she's trying to make that work. I think she's just fine, though Maria remains skeptical. I suspect there may be some woman-to-woman jealousy going on there, the young and shiny princess vs. the wise but older woman. Of course, I'll have to own up to some clouding of my own judgment as a middle-aged man enjoying attention from a beautiful younger woman.

Life.

Tonight, we're in Sittingbourne, in yet another parish hall: hard floors, no shower. After dinner, I tell the story of Dulcitius, from a play written by the nun Hrosvitha of Gandersheim in the 10th century. It's a comedy, if you can imagine, about a lecherous

Roman governor who tries to seduce three young virgins during the time of Diocletian's persecution of the Christians. The three sisters, Agape, Chionia, and Irena (Love, Purity, and Peace), resist his advances. He lures Agape into the kitchen to have his way with her, but the Holy Spirit descends to protect the daughter of Christ. Dulcitius's mind becomes clouded and while he thinks he's making out with Agape, he is really hugging and kissing the pots and pans. He emerges from the kitchen covered in grease and ash. As punishment for this deception, Dulcitius tries to burn the three sisters alive, but they're protected by God and it doesn't work. One can imagine the nuns at Gandersheim laughing and experiencing some titillation as they watched this play.

Our pilgrims have a similar response.

7 July

Four o'clock in the morning. People are spread out in the parish hall in Faversham. Very little feels private, especially when the sleeping arrangement are communal. There's a stage in the hall that the church must use for assemblies and Alice builds a fortress of chairs there to provide a buffer. Just before falling asleep, I hear David talking to his wife on the phone, lovingly encouraging her to meet us in London. Before that it's Al talking to his daughters, then Pete talking to his grandchild. Now the sounds of snoring and sneezing and farting echo through the hall as Rinnes's tail beats a steady rhythm against the hardwood floor anytime someone makes a trip to the loo.

Today's walk takes us to Gillingham, a very poor town south of London. We're in another parish hall, next to railroad tracks. The sound of the passing trains—every half hour—drowns out the sound of sleepers snoring and passing wind. Some of us go to a public swimming pool tonight, mostly to have a chance to take a shower. I end up leaving my good socks behind and I'm astounded at how much this annoys me—that's how important socks have become to me.

We have a fancy-ish dinner in town and take our leave of Father Giles, Pete, and Tomasz, who will all head back to Pluscarden tomorrow. Ann and Jo will then take over as cooks. Father Martin will assume liturgical and pastoral duties from Father Giles. He's joined by Brother Simon—a Polish monk at Pluscarden who is studying for the priesthood—who will walk with us for a few weeks. No one will replace Tomasz. Jo will drive instead.

8 July

We're waiting at the Town Pier in Gravesend. A boat has been chartered to take us up the Thames into London. David has grand plans for how this "entry of the pilgrims" will look.

6

London *to* Prinknash

8 July (continued)

Wherever we go, we carry our pilgrims' banner that displays Pluscarden Abbey's coat of arms. Rendered in the shape of a shield, this coat of arms dates from medieval times. The top register shows the cross of Saint Andrew, Scotland's patron saint, in white on a blue background, with two white stars on either side. The bottom register contains the head of a fire-breathing dragon with a human arm holding a cross jutting out of its mouth and extending into the left side of the shield. The picture is meant to represent Christ's victory over evil. The cross is literally helping humanity escape from the dragon's mouth.

We hang up this banner to signify and announce our presence, for example, from the gates of a parish hall where we're spending the night. I don't really know if anyone else knows or understands what the banner means, but it does create a kind of identity for the group, and it's easy to see from a distance. Turning a corner after a long day's trek, it's comforting to see our pilgrims' banner waving at the end of the road. At least you know you're not lost and that your walk is almost over.

Coat of arms from the Pluscarden 1230 Pilgrimage banner.

Now imagine this coat of arms flying from the mast of some quaint yaw or ketch or schooner, whose sails swell and billow before us, offering a silent and graceful entrance up the Thames into London. Or better yet, imagine a small galley or longship in which the pilgrims are the rowers, the act of rowing itself a kind of pilgrim's penance. Either of those scenarios might have left an impression, in dramatic contrast to the merchant ships and tourist ferries that comprise the regular traffic up and down the Thames. This is what I imagine when David tells me we'll be coming into London by boat, to the amazement of people all along the shore.

I am as much a romantic as David and this idea really appeals to me. But that's not how it goes. Instead, we board a speed boat christened the *Orion Clipper*. It's fast and sexy and fun, with the wind in our faces blowing our hair back on a gorgeous Saturday morning. Sadly, the boat ride into London has none of the impact David hoped for. To start with, there's no place onboard to hang our banner. The *Orion Clipper* is so fast that the banner would likely fly off. Easing into the dock, our luxury vessel must be delivering posh people to the shore, but none of any consequence. There's nothing that signals "pilgrims who've just walked across half of France for a worthy cause."

On top of that, it's Gay Pride weekend in London and the city is even more crowded than usual, if that's possible. Countless flamboyantly clad members of the LGBTQ community jostle along the pier and across the bridge at Westminster Cathedral. We arrive at Westminster Pier completely unnoticed, with none of the fanfare David had hoped to create, none of the "buzz" that would promote the Pluscarden 1230 Pilgrimage and its fundraising appeal. I'm disappointed for David's sake, but one of the things I like about him is his willingness, as Martin Luther used to say, to "sin boldly."

David's wife, Peta, is at the pier to greet us, as is Joe, whom we haven't seen since the priory at Vausse in France. Joe has connections at Westminster Cathedral and he very graciously organizes some comp tickets for a tour. I half expect him to tell me not to break anything when I go in, but Joe is ultimately too nice for that. The writer Harry Bucknall, on his own trek across the UK, is also there to greet us. Many of us have read Harry's book, *Like a Tramp, Like a Pilgrim*, about his pilgrimage to Rome, and found inspiration there.

9 July

We stay in a dorm in central London, the More House, connected to the Catholic Chaplaincy Centre at the University of London. We sleep four and five to a room with no air conditioning.

"Hey, it's a pilgrimage!" you might say. "What's your problem?" You're right, but it's hard to be present and contemplate God's plan in a room with no circulation on a hot and humid night in the middle of a city. Unless this was God's plan. Oh, bugger.

New pilgrims have arrived. One of them, a twenty-something soldier named Allan who's having trouble adjusting to army life, has joined the pilgrimage at his commander's recommendation. In Allan's words, he was "volunteered" for it. I think the commander's attitude is progressive, that the pilgrimage might be a way for someone to get his act together. But it also seems somewhat naïve, in terms of what to expect. Allan will only be with us for the week. Could the pilgrimage turn his life around in seven days? It didn't seem to work for Tomasz, and he was with us for five weeks. This is the same impulse that caused Andy the Spaniel's mother to sign him up, but it didn't seem to work for him.

Oh, so sorry for not catching you up. The Spaniel left us shortly after the wedding fiasco in Liesse-Notre-Dame and is currently touring Europe on a Eurail Pass. I think that's a much better way for an 18-year-old to spend his summer. What was his dear mother thinking?

10-12 July

We stay for three days at Douai Abbey in the Chiltern Hills, west of Reading. We've used this approach before: pick a home base in the middle of where the pilgrims will be walking, shuttle them to the starting point in the morning; fetch them at the RV point in the evening; and have a lot less stress packing up and pitching camp every day.

Contextual monastic history alert no. 1:

Douai Abbey was founded in 1615 in Paris, as a kind of daughter house to the famous monastery of Bury St. Edmunds in Suffolk. As such, it came under the patronage of Saint Edmund, the king and martyr. Edmund was killed by Danish Vikings in 869 for refusing to renounce his Christianity. A nasty Dane with the awesome moniker Ivar the Boneless ordered that Edmund be beaten, then shot with arrows, then beheaded. He still wouldn't renounce his faith, though I suppose that would be more difficult with no head. Ivar threw the faithful king's head into the forest, but his family was able to find it by following the voice of a wolf that kept repeating, "Over here. Over here." In any case, the Paris community became a spiritual and intellectual gathering place for monks from Bury St. Edmunds who were studying at the Sorbonne.

After the French Revolution and the dissolution of the monasteries, the Parisian monks regrouped in Douai, in northern France, and began training priests to serve Catholic populations in England and Wales. Further suppression of religious life came to France in the early 1900s, with its Laws of Association. France expelled the Douai community, but they took the name Douai to their new foundation at Upper Woolhampton in Berkshire, where we now find ourselves.

A big treat for me at Douai is its library: over 100,000 books, including medieval manuscripts and early printed works, as well as archives from Douai and other monasteries. The part of me that still loves traditional research wants to spend the rest of my summer here.

The guest house at Douai is a lovely cottage where we all sleep in real beds. Ann teaches some of us to make scones, but hers remain the best. I offer two stories at Douai. The first is the "Wife of Bath's Tale," from Chaucer, which we might characterize as an early "battle of the sexes" story. An old hag helps a knight and keeps him from being beheaded. (A lot of beheading in our narrative this week.) The knight promises to marry her, then balks because the woman is ugly. She offers him the choice: to have a beautiful wife who is unfaithful, or an ugly wife who will never betray her vows.

The second story I tell is the "Savage Pigs of Tulla," in which a farmer is eaten whole by his pigs. The quandary in this story is whether the villagers should kill the pigs and eat them, which—with the farmer still inside the pigs—suggests cannibalism, or inter the pigs entirely, so that the digested farmer can have a proper burial. Both stories generate great discussions and big questions about where true beauty lies, and where the soul resides.

13 July

We leave Douai for Faringdon, where we'll stay at the Blessed Hugh Catholic Church Hall, located on Marlborough Street across from the BETFRED off-site betting salon. Does the devil put these temptations in our path? Or is God trying to remind us of Jesus driving out the money changers?

We've actually already walked halfway to Faringdon, but we backtrack to Douai for our last night there. Jai and Jo have dropped us off somewhere in the woods between Farnborough and Wantage, between the Chiltern Hills and the North Wessex Downs. We should have an easy walk to Faringdon.

I think it will be easy, but I strain a tendon in the arch of my foot. Unbearably painful to put any weight on it. Mother f***! Jai takes me to the emergency room at the John Radcliffe Hospital in Oxford. I have to wait a little while to see the doctor, but not too long. In the triage of the ER, torn ligament in the foot is a pretty low priority. The doctor can't do anything but give me crutches, a couple of extra strength Tylenol, and a warning that the pilgrimage is over for me if I ever want to walk again without limping.

"No more pilgrimage," he says sternly.

"No, of course not," I say. "I'll rest up for the remainder of the summer." Yeah, right.

In any event, there are no charges for the services. Thank you socialized medicine. As a non-British citizen, a visitor to your country who has never paid into your system, I need help and you help me, no questions asked. Pay attention, America!

Most of the waiting I do during this whole fiasco is waiting for Jai to pick me up, which, because he's busy with other pilgrimage business, doesn't happen until the end of the day. Luckily, there's a Marks & Spencers outlet called "Simply Food" adjacent to the hospital, which has all manner of tasty delights. Again, the only pilgrimage in history where the pilgrims gain weight.

We stay tonight in a church hall in Faringdon. The church is beautiful in its own way. Built in 1840, it has rubblestone walls and large Gothic windows. During World War II, the church served as a canteen and movie theatre for troops stationed in the area. The accommodations are the usual: stake out a space on the floor and try not to let the snorers get to you.

14 July

We arrive today in Brownshill to overnight at the monastery of Our Lady and Saint Bernard.

Sitting alone in the cell the monastery has provided, I take time to ponder the "embodiment" of the pilgrimage. Much of my experience here is intellectual or spiritual, but—if it isn't too obvious to say so—I also experience the pilgrimage through my body. Aches and pains, sunburn and blisters, and that weird bite in its weird location, torn ligaments and flatulence and the smells a body makes when the only maintenance it's had for days has come from a bathroom sink. These are all part of the "embodiment" of pilgrimage, which could become a daily litany that eventually would cause you, dear reader, to throw this book into a fire. Please forgive me if this next admission is too forward, too blunt, too American, but occasionally I also feel randy. Maybe it's better to say that I'm longing for physical intimacy. At the same time, I feel too exhausted to act on that in any way.

Six weeks to go. Thank you for listening. We now return to our regularly scheduled pilgrimage.

15 July

Now at Prinknash Abbey, located near Cranham on the side of a valley in the Cotswolds. We're staying in the abbey's visitor centre, which also has an art gallery and an exhibit room with hand-carved models of medieval cathedrals and villages. This is where Maria has decided to sleep. The rest of us are sleeping in a meeting room next to the café. The worst temptation for all of us is sleeping next to a room with unlocked pastry cases.

Contextual monastic history alert no. 2

Why do we head west to Prinknash, rather than due north to Pluscarden?

Prinknash Abbey, Gloucester.

The history of Prinknash (rhymes with "spinach") is linked to Pluscarden's history. The Giffard family, which came to England with William the Conqueror, donated the land at Prinknash in 1096, to Abbot Serlo of the Benedictine Abbey of Saint Peter's in Gloucester. Most of the current building was constructed in the 1520s, under Abbot William Parker. In 1539, with the suppression of the monasteries, Henry VIII used Prinknash as a hunting lodge—echoes of Val-des-Choues. Prinknash was passed on through generations of the landed gentry, until 1928, when it was given to the monks of Caldey Island, off the southern coast of Pembrokeshire in Wales. The monks at Caldey had been Anglican, but they converted to Catholicism in 1913 under Abbot Ælred of Carlyle.

Six monks from Caldey came to Prinknash to transform it once again into a Benedictine monastery. In 1947, Prinknash founded two daughter houses, one at Farnborough and one that reclaimed Val-des-Choues's priory of Pluscarden. For these reasons, there are still close ties between Pluscarden and Prinknash.

Brother Simon has gone to the Isle of Wight for a workshop on Gregorian chant. He'll return to us next week. Meanwhile I've run into a monk at Prinknash—good friends with Brother Simon—who says we met when he was still at Pluscarden. He now makes incense at Prinknash, which is one of their main industries.

Allan, the troubled young soldier, leaves us early this morning. It's unclear whether this experience does him any good. He seems constantly connected to his phone and the internet, rather than talking with people or taking in nature. On the other hand, who knows what's helpful to one person and not another. He didn't do the pilgrimage the way I would have, but maybe in years to come he'll look back and find it was helpful, like students whom you think aren't getting anything out of your class and then come back years later to tell you how meaningful it was.

Ann is coming into her own on the pilgrimage. Like all of us, she has her quirks: non-sequiturs and partially expressed thoughts, spoonerisms and mixing up people's name. (She calls Jai, Al, and me, Pete.) She's an amazing cook, though I should probably say chef, with a real command of subtle flavors and an understanding of texture and presentation. It helps that most of the places we stay in the UK have kitchens, so Ann is not dependent on the crazy Army cooker that sometimes works and sometimes doesn't. As just one example, the kitchens we encounter give her the chance to bake.

Have I mentioned her scones?

7

Prinknash *to*
Melton Mowbray

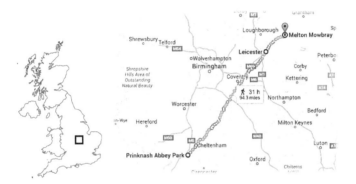

16 July

This is a group that reads. Maria has brought a huge suitcase of books with her and she keeps buying more books in charity shops along the way. She and the others are also generous in their attempts to expand my personal list to include some classics of British literature. My favorite recommendation from Maria is Jerome K. Jerome's late-19th-century comic travelogue, *Three Men in a Boat (to Say Nothing of the Dog)*, which Maria says I must read as soon as I can, perhaps as a model for what she's started calling "my pilgrimage book." Al offers up Laurie Lee's 1959 classic *Cider with Rosie*, about the author's experience growing up in England after World War I. The abbey at Prinknash is within driving distance of the home where Lee lived and wrote, so this afternoon Al purloins the keys to the van and takes me on a field trip. There's nothing more generous, I think, than sharing a book or a writer you love. A sign of true friendship.

On our last evening at Prinknash, I perform a mind-reading trick to the amazement of my fellow pilgrims. Having left the room, I am able to discern an object chosen by the audience when I'm not present. We play this game many times before anyone figures out that Al is acting as my confederate.

17 July

Saint Catharine Catholic Church, Chipping-Campden.

Today we walk to Chipping-Campden. We're camping in the courtyard of Saint Catharine's Church on the Lower High Street. The word "chipping" comes from an Anglo-Saxon word for "market." Chipping-Campden has indeed been a market town for centuries. Among other things, it was a centre of the medieval wool trade. The town's buildings have facades of locally-quarried, yellow limestone. One of the oldest and most important is the Market Hall, whose function was exactly as the name says.

Saint Catharine's was built in 1891 with support from the 2nd Earl of Gainsborough, whose conversion in the 1850s sparked a growth in Catholicism in Campden and the surrounding area. The community originally held services in the chapel of a Catholic school called Cow Fair. In 1891, the Earl paid to demolish an adjacent old barn and to build the new church.

Our host, Father Brennan, is a great talker, who regales us with many tales of the exorcisms he's performed. I'm skeptical, but it's interesting to see how some in the group—Ann, Maria, Father Martin—accept these stories uncritically. In a way, I'm envious that they are true believers.

18 July

Today we're in Stratford-upon-Avon. We have lodgings in the basement "function room" of the church of Saint Gregory the Great, a monastic parish run by monks from Douai. As we approach the rectory door, we spot a sleek, black Mazda Miata. Later we discover that this car belongs to the priest, who claims it was the most affordable car he could find. Hmm.

My foot is still acting up so I don't walk with the others. Instead, I do my own pilgrimage, on crutches, to see Shakespeare's tomb. Afterwards, I have a cup of tea at an outdoor café across from the theatre of the Royal Shakespeare Company. An attractive couple on holiday sits down next to me and I notice they're speaking French so I invite myself into their conversation. It's been two weeks since I've really spoken French and it's fun. After tea, I hobble over to the RSC and buy two tickets to that evening's production of *Antony and Cleopatra*, hoping that Maria will join me.

I haven't been taking many photos on this trip—part of my plan to be "in the moment"—but I take a photo of the RSC tickets and text it to my colleague who teaches Shakespeare, just to make him jealous.

Again, you might be asking, "what kind of pilgrimage was this, where you go to fancy theatre productions?"

All I can say is, "Lighten up." Pilgrimage and tourism have always been closely linked. In the Middle Ages, as today, commerce is connected to pilgrimage and vice-versa. Let me illustrate by explaining the origins of the word "tawdry."

Long-winded etymology alert:

First, in spite of any spiritual impulse, a pilgrimage is a journey. Journeys require food and lodging and even, dare I say, diversions. It's not surprising that Chaucer's story-telling contest is initiated by Harry Bailey, the tavern keeper at the Tabard Inn, a real place that welcomed real pilgrims starting in the early 14th-century. Bailey has already made some money from the Canterbury pilgrims' initial stop at the Tabard, and he stands to profit again upon their return from Canterbury to buy dinner for whomever has won the contest.

People on journeys also like souvenirs by which to remember their experiences. Pilgrims to the Holy Land would bring back palm fronds as proof that they'd made the journey. Hence, Chaucer calls pilgrims "palmers." Pilgrims to Santiago de Compostela wore scallop shells on their clothing for similar purposes. But there are palm fronds and scallop shells aplenty in these locations. How could other sites monetize the notion of bringing some of the pilgrimage back home?

Enter the clever vendors at the Shrine of Saint Audrey.

Audrey was an English princess in the 7th century. She married young but had sworn a vow of perpetual virginity. After three years, her husband died. She married again for political reasons, but the second husband wasn't so keen on her chastity vows. When he made advances upon her, she escaped to a monastery at Ely. Audrey died of a horrible tumor on her neck, which she interpreted as God's retribution for the vanity of her wearing so many beautiful necklaces in her youth.

Based on this story, medieval hawkers of merchandise began to sell lace necklaces at Saint Audrey's Fair, held every year on her feast day, and a great excuse for pilgrimage to Ely. By the 17th century, critics began to view the lace necklaces as shoddy and vulgar. They coined a new term to describe such cheap trinkets: "tawdry," a corruption of Sain-*t Audrey*.

So, yes. We went to see a play by one of the greatest writers to ever live at one of the greatest theaters in the world. Guilty. Tomorrow I will limp to Berkswell as penance.

19 July

In Berkswell, we're the guests of the vicar and curate of Saint John Baptist Anglican Church.

Saint John Baptist Anglican Church, Berkswell.

It's interesting that most of our hosts have been Catholic— local parishes, monastic communities—but this seems to be the first Protestant church. People here seem much more aware of doctrinal and denominational differences, nonetheless, these Anglicans are more than welcoming. The staff are very kind and the facilities are great. They invite us to join them for evening Vespers, which they conduct in a style very similar to the Benedictines—but just different enough that you can goof it up if you're not paying attention.

We have a great discussion after dinner about God and faith and religion. Al and Father Martin and I are the most vocal. As you might imagine, there is no unified school of thought, but everyone is being very direct and honest. Ann—who has great depth and sincerity but is often betrayed by her penchant for *non sequiturs*—asks about the meaning behind octagonal baptismal fonts, the Knights Templar, and the Cathar heretics, all of them seemingly connected in her mind. I do my best to answer.

<u>*Non sequitur* mini-lecture alert</u>:

> Christianity and the magical number 8. On the seventh day, God rested. In the Jewish tradition, this Sabbath is on Saturday, so, since Jesus rose on a Sunday, that would be the "eighth" day. Baptism is the start of eternal life. Resurrection comes through Jesus on day eight. So, eight sides. Or, if you like, there were eight souls who survived the flood in Noah's ark. We're all descended from them, so, eight sides. Or, here's the best one. According to Jewish law, Jesus was circumcised on the eighth day. Old Testament circumcision is roughly equivalent to New Testament baptism, so eight sides on the baptismal font.

Father Martin seems to smile and nod his approval of my explanation, but Ann's eyes glaze over. I tell her we'll get to the Templars another night, but the one thing she should know is that they were originally started as an order to protect pilgrims from being attacked on their way to the Holy Land.

20 July

"I couldn't begin to tell you what town we're in." That's what I wrote in my journal. Turns out it was Atherstone, a working-class town in Warwickshire. Overnight in a parish hall, Al sleeps with Rinnes in the handicapped loo. It's clean and has a door that locks. He claims it's the best night's sleep he's had, at least among the parish hall accommodations.

Another big discussion about religion. Jai calls native religions "weird" because they dress up in outrageous, colorful costumes. I reminded him that the pope does the same thing.

My only other note is that my foot is improving.

21 July

We're now at Mount Saint Bernard, a Cistercian abbey in Leicestershire, with private rooms and hot showers.

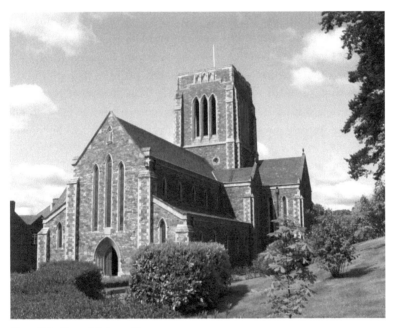

Mount Saint Bernard, Leicestershire.

Brother Simon has returned to us from his Gregorian chant workshop. He stays in the dormitory with the monks and offers to do all of our laundry in the monastery's communal washing machines. This is a great improvement over scrubbing socks and knickers in the sink. I lose a sock in the process. This is a regular occurrence, even doing laundry in my own home, but here it rises to the level of tragedy. Socks have become so important.

Jo is especially grateful for Brother Simon's offer to do the laundry because she has somehow become the group's *de facto* washer woman. I suppose this happened innocently enough when she had a small load and asked if anyone else had a few pieces to throw into the basket. Her kind offer was accepted by far too many of us and eventually it more or less became expected that Jo was doing our laundry because, well, she was doing laundry anyway. Eventually, she speaks up, in her gentle but direct way, and the matter somehow gets worked out.

No amount of gratitude can equal the work the support staff offers throughout the pilgrimage, but let me, once again sing the praises of Jo, Ann, Pete, Tomasz, Jai, and David. Heroes all!

The homily at Mass this morning at Mount Saint Bernard is all about the evils of sodomy, which is the priest's way of railing against homosexuality. It's interesting how conservative most people I encounter on the pilgrimage seem to be, at least about social and sexual issues. Maybe I'm just responding from the liberal "bubble" of my insulated university mindset.

22 July

Our destination for the weekend is Melton Mowbray. At 22 miles, it's one of our longest hikes. This means nothing to Al and some of the more fit walkers, but I only make it halfway on my still improving foot before I call Jai for a ride.

Chris wants to see the movie *Dunkirk*, which has just opened this weekend. Several of us pile into the van. Chris drives and I navigate. We pull out of the parking lot of our lodgings and as we barrel down the road, something doesn't feel right. Chris is driving on the right side of road, which is to say the *wrong* side of the road. We're back in the UK and we should be on the *left*! We left France two weeks ago so it's odd that Chris hasn't made the transition. He actually argues with me for a bit as I try to point this out to him. Cresting a hill, he makes the adjustment seconds before driving us head-on into a bus full of tourists.

During the first week of the pilgrimage, David admitted to me that his biggest fear was a massive wipeout of pilgrims on a busy street—but he meant while we were walking, not driving! Thanks be to God, tragedy averted.

We make it into the city and get tickets for *Dunkirk*. As a film student, Chris is a big fan of the director, Christopher Nolan, so he seems more like an excited little kid than he normally does. I sit next to Al, who as an RAF pilot has seen combat, though he resists talking about it. All during the movie, I watch Al out of the corner of my eye, as he watches the aerial fight scenes. At the end of the movie, I find myself thinking of my grandfather, for whom I'm named. He was a reconnaissance photographer on a bomber crew during the war, flying many missions over Germany. I start to cry. but stop as the lights come up in the theater.

8

Melton Mowbray
to Ampleforth

23 July

Towns are starting to meld together, one into the next. An entire two-page spread in my journal is blank except for the phrase "What happened here?!" Sometimes, I'm too wiped to journal at the end of every day, so events and memories get lost. Monday morning, we leave Melton Mowbray for … no idea. Maybe Grantham? That's halfway between Melton Mowbray and Lincoln and I'm pretty sure we're in Lincoln on Tuesday. Without better notes, my memory gets fuzzy. Wednesday we're in Market Rasen and Friday is my birthday, which we celebrate in Market Weighton. But it's 40 miles from Market Weighton to Ampleforth, too far to walk in one day at our pilgrims' pace. We must have stopped somewhere in between. York? Maybe we walked some and drove some to move things along. This would make sense if that's how David had to set up the lodging. I know we visited York Minster, but it's not in my journal.

Oh, bloody hell. Next pilgrimage: take better notes.

In any case, I'm walking again on a regular basis, but my foot is still causing problems. I usually make it about half the scheduled distance before calling Jai for a ride. If the day's walk is for eighteen miles, I do nine. I'm trying to take it easy and not let my ego get in the way.

24 July

Grantham. I pause in front of an impressive church named for St. Wulfram (above), a missionary to the Frisians who died in 702

AD. The Frisians sacrificed their own people to appease their pagan gods, a custom that Wulfram found distasteful. He finally won them over when he saved a man named Ovon from being sacrificed by hanging. The Frisians watched as Wulfram prayed over Ovon's dangling body for several hours. As soon as the Frisians decided to leave Ovon for dead, the rope snapped and, miraculously, he was still very much alive. The Frisians accepted Wulfram's god as more powerful and converted on the spot to Christianity. For his part, Ovon went on to become a monk.

25 July

Lincoln. A very nice priest welcomes us to his parish hall. Good lodgings, except that the floor is hard and cold. This is one of those arrangements that was sorted at the last minute, but it all works out.

Chris has returned from a couple of days working on another film project—a paid gig. It feels good to have him back, like the group is complete. We learn that Father Martin and Brother Simon will be leaving next week, heading back to Pluscarden. Father Mark, whom I don't think I've ever met, will join us for spiritual support.

I think back on all my fretting early on about transitions impacting the group dynamic. Blah, blah, blah. Now I'm embarrassed to say that I hardly give a thought to the Spaniel, or Tomasz, or others who so occupied my thoughts in the first couple of weeks. Am I just a self-centered jerk? Is this a product of living in the moment? Does the daily routine—pack, eat, walk, eat, unpack, sleep—take up so much energy that names and faces fade? The "new" is so intense, all-consuming really. But does anyone else, other than those of us in this moment, really care about what we're doing? Is there still a unified vision of what all this walking and intentional living together means? Or is this all existential angst as my 59th birthday approaches?

I'm tired of the lack of privacy, though we all do our best to respect each another's space. Today on the walk, Maria tells me that she's been holding back so that we could walk together. Chris assures her that I like walking alone. He's right.

I start to think of the pilgrimage as representing the two forms of monastic life: the eremitic (hermit's life) and the coenobitic (community life). I get to have my eremitic experience when I'm on the road alone, moving at my own pace and letting my thoughts go where they will. Then in the evening and the next morning, I'm in the coenobitic life, where Saint Basil said we get to practice Christian charity.

As Chris and Maria pull away, I think how comforting it is to see them in the distance, sometimes the far distance. As long as I can see them, there's a fifty-fifty chance that I'm not lost. It's also funny to hear them talk about spotting me far behind them, only to realize that they're seeing the white top of a bus rather than my white hair.

26 July

Accommodations in the rectory at Holy Rood church in Market Rasen are very nice, except that our host, Father Robert, smokes heavily and everything reeks of cigarettes. Wake up hacking.

27 July

Almost lost another day to bad memory and lazy note taking. At first I think we must have stayed in Barton-upon-Humber because my journal says that a group of pilgrims walked across the one-and-a-half mile Humber Bridge, but that's not right.

Al tells me that the Humber Bridge was the longest single-span suspension bridge in the world when it was first built, in 1981, and held that record until 1998, when it was surpassed by a bridge in Japan. Several pilgrims say that the view from the middle is quite dramatic. I don't get to see it because I stay home to nurse a cold—it isn't the smoker's air at the rectory, I do indeed have a chest cold. My body continues to betray me on this trip. As for the Humber

Bridge, Chris assures me that I didn't miss anything, but this could be the cynicism of youth speaking.

Now it's come to me: we're in Hessle (north of the River Humber, not south of the river in Barton), in the parish hall at Our Lady of Lourdes.

Tonight at dinner, Ann reports many adventures from her day. She and Jo are now walking with the pilgrims, rather than just being tied to the kitchen. They put in a few hours a day. It's not only healthy physically, but I think it helps them feel more connected to the group, rather than just being "servants." Others have pitched in with the meal prep as much as possible. A sudden rain catches them off guard today, so they pop into a charity shop to find cheap replacements for their drenched clothing. Maria then tells us how she had followed Ann and Jo into the same charity shop after they'd gone. She overhears the shop keepers gossiping about the pilgrims who had "walked all the way from France and hadn't brought any waterproof gear." Then Maria introduces herself as a pilgrim. The dinner audience bursts into laughter.

Ann also has an encounter with a baker in town, whom she wants to marry because of his extensive knowledge of historical pastries. She brings home treats called "Maids of Honors," basically a lemon tart in a puff pastry shell. According to Ann's most knowledgeable baker and future spouse, Henry VIII gave the pastries their name because that's what Ann Boleyn and her maids were enjoying the first time he met them.

"You see," Ann says, looking right at me. "All of us can be teachers."

"I absolutely agree," I say. "Thanks for the lesson."

28 July

We're in Market Weighton, east of York, in the parish hall of Our Lady of Perpetual Help. Seems like the perfect place for my birthday. Ann and Jo have been pestering me all week about what they should cook for this occasion. I throw them a curve ball and tell them that I would like to cook.

The menu consists of smoked salmon and caviar for starters. Then comes a "washtub salad," basically every vegetable and fruit under the sun with mixed greens in a honey mustard vinaigrette. Ann and Jo provide birthday cake in the form of chocolate covered pastries.

Until now, I had been telling the after-dinner stories, so, since it's my birthday, I ask them to tell me a story. They're all nervous and don't believe they can do it. Jai is especially resistant. I teach them the "one-word story" game, in which each person in the circle tells a snippet of the story, then going around the circle the next in line has to continue the tale, until everyone has had a turn. Jai happens to be sitting to my left, so I say that he should go first.

He pauses for a long time, gives me a few nasty looks, then begins. I wish I could tell you what his story is about, but he performs the entire bit in Nepalese—and I do mean *performs*. He uses gestures and facial expressions and inflection. It's thrilling. Even though none of us understand a word he says, we can somehow follow along and get where he is in the story. Jai stops and turns to Ann, sitting next to him. She also pauses for a long time and says she "can't speak that language that Jai was speaking."

"No worries," I say. "Just continue as best you can."

Ann picks it up and the story becomes about butterflies, then Maria adds in a princess, then Brother Simon adds whatever he adds, and then Al and Chris and Father Martin and all the rest. I've no idea anymore what the story is about, but it's so much fun watching them put it together, showing different, sillier, and also deeper sides of themselves. The story comes back around to Jai and he finishes, again in Nepalese, this time with songs and Nepalese dance gestures and a moral translated into English. Ann adds the coda at the end, with the most deadpan comic delivery:

"And they all drowned."

Lots of laughing and silliness.

29 July

We do stop in York.

I take the tour of the Cathedral and Metropolitan Church of Saint Peter in York, known to most people as York Minster. Every square inch deserves description, but I would soon run out of superlative adjectives. One thing that captures my attention for a goodly while is the so-called Kings' Screen that separates the cathedral's choir and sanctuary from its nave. The screen has fifteen life-sized statues of English kings, from William the Conqueror to Henry VI.

Kings' Screen, York Minster Cathedral, York.

Historical rumination alert:

What fascinates me the most is the iconography chosen for each king. Let me focus on the eight kings in the register to the right of the choir's entrance.

Henry III holds two sceptres. Edward I holds a sword. Edward II and III both hold single sceptres, but Richard II goes back to just a sword. Henry IV and V both opt for sceptre and sword, while Henry VI takes things in a new direction, holding a sceptre and book, which he nonchalantly reads from his pedestal on the Kings' Screen. In the iconography of such depictions, a sceptre is always a sign of sovereignty or royal authority. The word "sceptre" comes from the Greek verb *skeptein*, meaning "to prop oneself up." Kings being "propped up." Funny.

A sword means power but also wisdom—think Solomon dividing the baby in two. A book means learning. No surprise with that last one. I don't know enough about the royal history of England to know why each king is holding his particular set of objects. (My helpful editor later informs me that Henry VI is considered England's first scholar-king, hence the book he's holding.)

As I walk away from the screen, I recall that I'm carrying a coin in my pocket from the reign of Henry III (1216-1272). It's M. Monot's coin that's making a round trip from Val-des-Choues to Pluscarden and back. I take the coin out and look at it. My numismatic skills are rusty, but I venture this is a "long cross penny" because of the image of the cross on the reverse of the coin (the back side). The obverse (front side) has a picture of Henry III but it's stylized and flattened out and bears no resemblance to the very lifelike statue before me. Oh, well.

Leaving York Minster, we walk York's market streets. Lots of buskers out. One guy who is quite impressive plays the cello while manipulating a puppet that plays a puppet-sized cello. On one level, his coordination leaves me scratching my head, but there's also a fanciful *poésie* at work here.

Al turns us on to Betty's Tea Room. They serve amazing pastries, of course, but the feature that Al, the former RAF pilot, wants to share is a giant mirror in Betty's basement, on which RAF pilots during World War II scratched their names before heading out on their missions.

"You see," Ann says. "We can all of us be teachers."

I smile.

It's the weekend again, so we'll stay for two nights in Ampleforth Abbey and College. This is a huge monastic complex, which includes a boys' school. While we're there, Ampleforth is in the news for its involvement in the Church's worldwide sexual abuse scandal and subsequent cover up.

This news has a huge impact on the Pluscarden monks traveling with us. Although their religious life is contemplative rather than active (i.e., they don't teach in schools), they nonetheless feel shock, disbelief, shame, embarrassment, and a little defensiveness. The overall percentage of clergy involved in the scandal is small. This isn't an excuse for those who are guilty, but it must be tough to get lumped in with the "bad clergy," when there are so many "good clergy" out there.

In 2009, the Vatican put out a statement that 5% or less of clergy worldwide had been involved in the scandal over the last 50 years. They presented this as comparable to clergy in other denominations. A study commissioned by the Church found that this number was significantly less than the overall male population, but that study was methodologically flawed. *Newsweek* reported that the numbers among Catholic clergy were about the same as for men overall.

This is all meaningless to the children and families involved in this horrific crime, and it probably seems odd to include such a topic in this jolly travelogue of our summer pilgrimage. The heaviest subjects discussed thus far have been sore feet and uncomfortable bedding. This is to say that the problems of the world don't vanish when one goes on pilgrimage, any more than they vanish if one joins a monastery. Pilgrims and monks do not escape from life. It follows them, as it follows us all.

9

Ampleforth *to*
Alnwick Castle

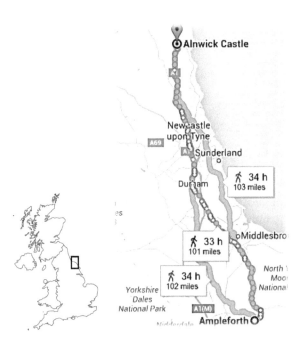

30 July

Sunday at Ampleforth. Transitions. Father Martin and Brother
Simon are relieved by Father Mark and Brother Michael. New
pilgrims arrive: David and Steve, both from Elgin, in Scotland, and
Mike, from Austin, Texas, just north of where I grew up. Steve
plays the fiddle and gives us a sample as soon as he arrives. Nothing

against the bagpipes, but this is more to my taste. Joe has also returned.

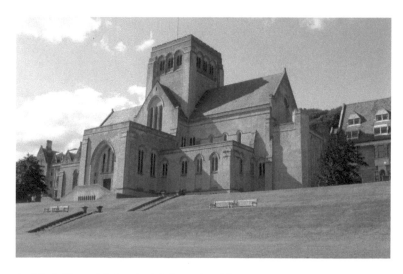

Ampleforth Abbey and College, Ampleforth, North Yorkshire.

Sunday after Mass. I take a long walk with Jo in the woods around Ampleforth. It's the anniversary of her husband's death (or close to it), and she weeps visibly during the Mass. I'm sitting next to her in the pew, so I put my hand on her back to offer some comfort. It turns out she's a member of a charismatic renewal group, into faith healing and exorcisms. She says she feels a "power" coming through my hand and asks if I've ever considered becoming a healer. Such beliefs are puzzling to me and I'm never sure how to respond with respect and skepticism at the same time.

31 July

We're staying in the Old Hall, which sits atop a wooded hill in Osmotherly, a village in North Yorkshire. Founded in 1665 by Lady Juliana Walmsley, the Old Hall was meant to support pilgrims visiting Osmotherly's Lady Chapel. It's been raining all day, so the drive up the hill is a bit treacherous and one of the vans has to be pulled out of the mud.

The Old Hall is a lovely two-story cottage with a fireplace in the dining room, which we have blazing even though it's late July. Elizabeth Walmsley (a descendant of Juliana?) visits us just before dinner and brings a good bottle of Scotch whiskey "to warm us up." Elizabeth tells us the story of an ornate cross that stands in the Lady Chapel. Apparently, before the start of World War II, a Scottish woman who belonged to the parish in Osmotherly saw it in an antique shop and asked the dealer how much it cost. The shop owner replied that the woman could have the cross if she helped his Jewish family escape Nazi Germany.

Before she goes, Elizabeth invites all of the pilgrims to stop by her cottage the next morning for tea and scones. She explains that her place is just at the bottom of the hill after exiting the woods. She promises to hang a Union Jack on her front gate, so we'll be able to identify it.

By the time I show up, three other pilgrims are already there, but Elizabeth still has plenty of scones and tea. I stay a bit longer than my three companions and Elizabeth shows me her art collection, which she's acquired from travels all over the world. She's a lovely and charming hostess, which is why it's such a shame that Joe and Maria don't get to meet her again.

It's never good when the two worst map readers in the group decide to walk together on such a regular basis. Luckily, neither Joe nor Maria sees this as a deficit, since they always seem to end up having fantastic adventures. Remember Elizabeth Walmsley's directions to the pilgrims: as you exit the forest, at the bottom of the hill, look for the Union Jack hanging from the front gate. What could be easier? But there's more than one exit point from the forest surrounding the Old Hall, and, at least on this particular morning, more than one patriotic cottage in Osmotherly hanging the Union Jack from its front gate. Joe and Maria find the other one. Here's how they tell their story.

Knock-knock-knock. A man comes to the front door. Joe points over his shoulder to the Union Jack and says, "We're pilgrims."

"Yes?" the man says.

"We're pilgrims," Joe says.

"Yes?"

"Your wife invited us over for scones."

The man hesitates. It's not beyond comprehension that his wife would invite pilgrims over for scones and not tell him.

"Honey," he says down the hallway into the house. "The pilgrims are here for tea and scones."

"What?"

At this point, the wife apparently can't remember if she's invited any pilgrims for tea. She might have. She doesn't have scones, but tea is no bother. Somehow, everyone now feels so committed to this event—no matter how unplanned—that Joe and Maria stay for tea and have a lovely chat with these kind Osmotherly villagers. In the end, their error is revealed, but everyone has a good laugh. Joe even claims that they exchange addresses in order to send Christmas cards.

1 August

We arrive in Stockton-on-Tees, where the parishioners of the Church of the English Martyrs and Saints Peter & Paul will be taking care of us. The women of the church are preparing a three-course meal, but first we'll be taken to our lodgings in private homes for a shower, after which we'll return to the presbytery for dinner.

Jai, Maria, and I are staying with a doctor from Poland named Mariszka (attractive, roughly 40 years old), who tells us right away she's a control freak. Sure enough, as soon as we set foot in her home, she bosses us around in a most loving way in order to help us relax and regenerate.

"Lie down," she commands, pointing me towards a sofa. "Eat," she says and gestures to a huge platter of fresh fruit, cheeses, and nuts. "Put your feet up. Drink water. Close your eyes." This is insanity, I think, though it all feels good and it's only the beginning. While Jai is taking a bath upstairs and I'm lying on a sofa in the living room, Mariszka gives Maria a foot rub in her study. Remember, she's a medical doctor, so this foot rub has to be amazing. Indeed, I hear Maria moan and purr with approval from the next room. When Jai is done with his bath, Maria goes upstairs. Mariszka comes into the living room.

"Come," she says to me. "I rub your feet."

"Oh, no thank you," I say. "My feet are too ticklish."

"I give you back rub."

"Uh …"

"Come, take off shirt."

Surely this is taking Jesus's commandment to "serve the neighbor" a bit far. Yet, it seems Mariszka's commandment must also be obeyed. So, I "take off shirt." She gives me a fantastic backrub, but my brain is short-circuiting. "Take off shirt. I give you backrub," is a set of instructions I normally receive in a context that evokes certain expectations. I don't think the good doctor wants anything more, and Jai and Maria are both right here, but this is more intimacy than I'm used to with someone I've known for less than an hour.

Finally, it's my turn for a bath. I soak until Mariszka knocks on the bathroom door to tell me we have to leave for dinner. Thank God she doesn't come in. She gives us all a ride back to the presbytery for dinner but doesn't stay.

The dinner is superb. The church ladies have pulled out all the stops. There are three different starters, plus a salad, then baked ham for the main course and two kinds of cake for dessert, not to mention fruit and cheese. They refuse to let us get up and serve ourselves and won't let us clear the table or help with the washing up. We're unworthy of so much kindness.

There are other guests at the dinner, the parish priest and some church elders. No other women are at the table—they're only in the kitchen. Jo, happy to not be cooking on this night, is sitting next to some guy she's met before. I think she introduces him as a priest and exorcist. Jo tells the priest about my "healing hands." He begins to encourage me to pursue studies in "Christian renewal." Jo tells me that she speaks in tongues and has participated in exorcisms. She is a true believer, which I respect, even when I don't understand it. I'm not a believer. Again, I can't figure out how to respond.

Thankfully, Steve brings out his fiddle and starts to play. He seems only to know jigs, but no one is dancing. I take the initiative and invite one of the church ladies to join me. She looks to be about 80, so I assume I'll need to be gentle, but she holds her own.

Mariszka returns and takes Maria, Jai, and me back to the soft beds she's prepared for us. Separate bedrooms. I try to repay Mariszka's kindness by cooking breakfast next day for her and the others, though it's clear that she may implode from having to let someone be nice to her. In spite of her rather stern, Eastern-European demeanor, she gives me a big hug and kiss on the cheek when we leave.

2 August

Father Mark has been taking photos along the pilgrimage, but today he forgets his camera on the beach. Brother Michael and I help him look for it, but without success.

The walking goes well. My foot is cooperating. We stay in a parish hall at the church of Saints Peter and Paul in South Shields. I don't recall anything extraordinary happening there, except for my intense disappointment that we won't have time to visit the Bede Museum at Jarrow Hall in the town of Jarrow. The venerable Bede, a medieval monk who wrote *The Ecclesiastical History of the English People*, is considered the patron saint of historians.

Oh, well. Next time. This can't become a travelogue of all the things we didn't do. We're just so close ... nerdy, academic longing. (I need Steve to play some pining lament on his fiddle.)

3 August

We walk to Minsteracres, a Christian retreat centre: woods all around, bunk beds, a big, well-outfitted kitchen, and a roaring fireplace—again, in August?!

Richard, one of the pilgrims from week 2, shows up with his wife for a visit. It's been over a month and everyone is happy to see Richard and to meet his wife, who is just as warm as he is. Plus, they bring baked goods—Richard knows our weaknesses. Some of the pilgrims ask me to tell a story, but I'm not in the mood. I feel myself more and more thinking of the quiet of home. I tell the gang that I'll work on a story for tomorrow.

Minsteracres Retreat Centre, Northumberland.

4 August

Still at the retreat centre and Al is anxious to get going. The bigger the group, the more out of the way our accommodations, the harder it is to get things going in the morning. This is especially true when we don't start our hike from the lodgings but have to get dropped off.

Today's walk is mostly along the shore. The salt air feels good. Maria and I talk about relationships. Honestly, I don't know if it's being on pilgrimage, or the intense closeness of our communal experiment, or if it's just this mix of people, but folks who barely knew each other at the beginning of the summer are having deep discussions. Maria asks me questions about my own experiences. She's roughly a decade older than me. She's had a couple of husbands and has ten kids. After exhausting that topic, we chat about watching *Antony and Cleopatra* at the Royal Shakespeare Company. The conversation rambles as much as the paths we're on.

We end the day in the parish hall at Saint Aidan's church in Ashington. I tell the story of "Gawain and the Green Knight." No one over-interprets the story and sees themselves being challenged by a giant to a head-lopping contest. After dinner, I try to explain Abbot and Costello's "Who's on first?" comedy routine to Ann, since most conversations with her seem to have that feeling.

"Costello is Jo's last name," she says. "Are you trying to say something about Jo?"

"No," I say. "Costello is also the name of the ... Never mind."

5 August

The walk to Alnwick Castle is 21 miles. I'm feeling fit, but not that fit. I ask Jai to pick me up around lunchtime near Hadston, which is about halfway there. He drives me to Alnwick and I help the support staff set up.

10

Alnwick Castle
to Edinburgh

6 August

We spend two nights at Alnwick (pronounced AN-ick) Castle, which gives us great accommodations: private rooms with locks on the doors, clean white linens, laundry facilities, and a large kitchen and dining room, just right for the size of our group this week. We mark 1,000 miles at Alnwick and, of course, we have cake to celebrate the occasion.

These days, Alnwick is best known as the location for scenes of the Hogwarts school in two *Harry Potter* movies: *Philosopher's Stone* and *Chamber of Secrets*. Speaking of Thomas Becket, the castle also served as a set for Richard Burton's eponymous film of 1964, as well as Kevin Costner's 1991 *Robin Hood: Prince of Thieves*, arguably the first movie where Robin has a Midwestern American accent. On the smaller screen, Alnwick Castle has served as a set for everything from *The Black Adder* to *Star Trek: The Next Generation* to *Downton Abbey*.

I'm surprised to find out that Saint Cloud State University, just an hour from my home in Minneapolis, runs an exchange program in Alnwick Castle. In fact, the director of that program is now a dean where I used to teach. Small world.

Alnwick Castle, Alnwick.

Joe returns to the pilgrimage, as does Robbie. Al's two daughters, Joanna (17) and Sarah (15), also join us this week. Al's home life must be full of laughter and practical joking, at least that's how he presents himself with his daughters.

For their introduction to the group, Al concocts a strange set of ritualistic sayings and gestures, ending with everyone sitting in a circle and patting the head of the person sitting next to them. We do this instead of saying grace at lunch. Al wants to see if his kids will politely observe, actively try to follow along, or shake their heads because they know this must be their dad's foolishness. One of the daughters plays along once we get to the head patting. The other resists and asks her father what kind of creepy cult he's brought them to.

Al also commissions a story for his daughters for after dinner. I devise a tale of two medieval sisters trying to win their knightly father's love. Al tells me to name the sisters in the story "Favorite Child" and "Such a Disappointment," which are apparently names he uses when discussing his daughters *in their presence*, regularly changing which name goes with which daughter. As soon as the daughters hear these names in the story, they realize the whole thing is going to be about them. They glare lovingly at their dad, wondering what other personal or family details he has shared.

The highlight of our stay in Alnwick is not the castle, which is pretty amazing, but a visit to Barter Books, a re-purposed train station converted to a used bookstore. A miniature train actually runs overhead through the entire store. It's a charming atmosphere, with lots of comfy reading chairs and a fine collection, housing many first editions, even comic books. I buy a copy of *Three Men in a Boat*, which makes Maria happy since she recommended it almost three weeks ago.

Maria makes not one, but two trips to Barter Books. We joke that she keeps buying books during this pilgrimage, which we're basically hauling around through France and England. Maria's friend Kevin, who's in the House of Lords, is visiting and he promises to drive Maria's books to Scotland so they won't "take up space" on the pilgrimage.

7 August

The walkways and stairs at Alnwick Castle have not been upgraded to meet modern building codes. Coming down a well-worn set of stone steps, Maria takes a tumble. I'm walking in front of her when I hear a rumbling sound from behind—it's Maria's suitcase, loaded with books. I jump out of the way and look back up the stairs in time to see Maria following the downward path of her luggage. Dumb luck and the remnants of once quick reflexes allow me to grab Maria's arm as she rushes by, headfirst. She hurts her back but avoids splitting her skull open.

We walk along the shore again, past the coastal towns of Seahouses, Bamburgh, and Belford. We're in a parish hall tonight, but I have no idea where. The variation in the comfort levels of our accommodations is starting to hit home for me. From one day to the next, we sleep on cold hard floors or comfy beds with sheets that smell like springtime. We either have showers with endless hot water or take what folks in my family used to call a "naval douche"—stand at the sink, take care of the face and armpits and hope that the good woolen underwear will last one more day.

8 August

Pilgrims crossing in Scotland.

Berwick-upon-Tweed. I buy a couple of shirts for the cooler weather we anticipate, once we cross into Scotland. I also get a haircut, mostly for the luxurious feeling of having someone shampoo my hair. The most important thing about Berwick-upon-Tweed, for the pilgrims at least, is that it's our last stop in England before crossing into Scotland. For the Scots in our party, this was like arriving at the promised land. The Scottish border is the starting point for today's walk. The pilgrims linger there for maybe 20 minutes, taking selfies and group photos. Everyone asks everyone else to take a picture of them with their phones. There is no irony in any of their expressions of joy. I try to recall if I've ever felt that way upon returning to my homeland. Not in quite the same way, I think.

9-10 August

We spend two nights in Nunraw Abbey in Hadington and organize the walks from this single home base.

Contextual monastic history alert no. 3:

> The name Nunraw (literally, "nun's row") reveals that the monastery was originally a convent for nuns. It was founded by Ada de Warenne, a 12th-century Scottish princess. Nunraw was shut down in the wake of John Knox's 16th-century reforms. When it was re-dedicated in 1946, it became the first Cistercian monastery in Scotland since the Reformation. Today Nunraw is home to Trappists, a subset of Cistercians who claim to practice a stricter observance of the *Rule of Saint Benedict*.

The men sleep among the stacks in Nunraw's library. This is dangerous because, as I've said, ours is a group of people who like to read. I witness many a camping head torch illuminating late-night explorations of Nunraw's collection. For their part, the female pilgrims sleep in a kind of meeting room and have to make do with whatever books they've brought with them.

I barely avoid a full-on meltdown today. I get left behind at the RV point because Jai's Land Rover doesn't have enough room for all the pilgrims he needs to fetch. It feels like I'm always the one being left behind and having to wait for others. (I write "abandoned" in my journal, but that now feels too dramatic.) When Jai finally comes back to get me, it turns out that he's only transferring me to a car park, *where everyone else is waiting for me*. I feel ridiculous for getting so angry, but I also find it difficult to let that anger go.

11 August

We arrive at a parish hall in Musselburgh, though I can't tell you which church. Places and events are once again starting to blur together. We're on the floor again, but with only five guys in a space the size of a tennis court, the sleeping arrangements seem luxurious. I've no idea where/how the women sleep.

My foot is giving me trouble again, so I take the day off from walking and work with Jo instead. After food shopping and errands, we drive into Edinburgh for a couple of hours. Even though we're going to be in Edinburgh the next day, it's only twenty minutes by car, so, why not? She talks about her life as a widow and whether or not she might marry again. She's doubtful. I suggest that it's still pretty soon after her husband's death.

Even after such a pleasant outing, with gorgeous weather and good company, I get back to Musselburgh and sink into a serious funk. I'm ready to be done, ready to go home. I hope it will feel different next week, with just the core group. We'll see.

Falling asleep, I listen to the call and response of snores, seeking comedic harmony.

12 August

We're staying in a parish hall in Edinburgh, in a neighborhood called Morningside that's within walking distance of Edinburgh's Old Town. Please understand that a phrase like "walking distance" takes on a different meaning when you've been on pilgrimage as long as we have. I'd guess it's about a 45-minute walk from where we're staying to where the action is.

Edinburgh for the weekend! I've been here four or five times before, with and without students, so it feels quite familiar to me: the castle, the Royal Mile, the Woolen Mill. We arrive in the middle of the Fringe Festival, so the streets are crowded with people watching the many free performances on almost every inch of Edinburgh's shopping streets and city parks. We all go to dinner at a Chinese place Chris has found online. Chris doesn't join us—says he has a date. There's sure to be lots of teasing for him at some point. Lots of good fellowship at dinner, saying goodbye to the pilgrims who will leave us tomorrow. Then we splinter off to find whatever evening's entertainment we desire.

11

Edinburgh *to* Luss

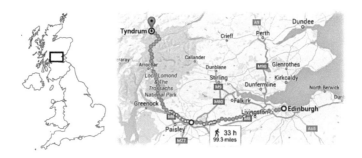

13 August

Edinburgh, the morning after. Not too much late-night activity for me yesterday. Chris even returns to the parish hall at a reasonable hour. Father Martin rejoins us and everyone is glad to see him. Joanna and Sarah, Al's lovely daughters, leave us today. It's obvious they've had a good time and we'll miss them.

14-15 August

We spend two nights in the parish hall at St Anthony's Catholic Church, on the outskirts of Falkirk. The medievalist in me immediately thinks of the Battle of Falkirk in 1298, where Edward I finally defeated William Wallace (Braveheart).

On the way to the drop-off point we drive by the Kelpies at Helix Park, two gigantic metal statues of horse heads dramatically rising out of the landscape.

16 August

We're in Glasgow, staying in Turnbull Hall, a large dormitory building of the Catholic Chaplaincy at the University of Glasgow. About a year ago, I met study abroad reps from Glasgow. They gave me a fine silver pen, one of those giveaways with the university logo on it. It's an excellent pen that I'm actually using at this very moment to write in my journal.

The men are camped on the floor of a large meeting room. The women are in one end of another large space, which has a dining room and kitchen. The kettle is on for tea. Ann and Jo have "gotten the messages" (done the shopping), so a tin of assorted biscuits sits on the dining room table, where Maria has broken out the portable Scrabble game. I sit down to join in. Ann and Jo are playing as a team. Jai partners up with Father Martin.

Al's wife, Sandy, comes for an afternoon visit. She's attractive and intelligent, as we expect. The two of them watch us play Scrabble as we watch them, trying to discern what kind of relationship they might have. Sandy is a successful doctor. Al has spent his life in the RAF, often stationed in faraway places. Somehow they've managed to raise two beautiful daughters, who seem headed for good universities and accomplished lives.

17 August

I have a lovely walk with Maria on our way to the pilgrimage centre in Luss. We divert from the path to walk along the western shore of Loch Lomond, Scotland's largest lake, which lies at the southern edge of the Highlands. Hiking south to north, we see rolling, tree-covered hills and small islands followed by rugged mountains. Any adjective I can think of is unworthy to the task of describing the scenery "on the bonnie, bonnie banks o' Loch Lomond."

Eventually we come into some thick forest and have to fight our way through. We emerge on the other side at ... a golf course?!

Yep. There it is on the map. We come to realize that we've landed right in the middle of the Loch Lomond Golf Club, a super-exclusive establishment where members must be nominated by other members and where "conveniently located" means "less than 90 minutes flight from London, 2 hours from Paris and approximately 6 hours from New York and Dubai." Trying to find our way out, we come to a building in the middle of the grounds. Its small parking lot is packed with BMWs and Jaguars and Mercedes and a few cars that are so posh I don't recognize their brands. The building turns out to be the club spa, which is located inside a walled garden designed by Thomas White in 1797. We walk in to get directions.

"We've gotten lost," I say. "Does this road lead back to the main highway?"

"Yes, yes," says an efficient hostess seated at a marble-top table in front of cherry paneling. We thank her and leave, but not before Maria spies a sign advertising massages.

"How much?" Maria asks.

"£100."

"Thank you." We walk out the door, but Maria stops.

"Should we?"

I smile.

We go back in and ask the hostess about available times. She finds two spots that will only put us 90 minutes behind schedule. Oh, my God, this will be so worth it after being on the road all summer. Part of me thinks I should save something like this for the end of the pilgrimage—just as Chaucer's pilgrims would have done? And didn't I already have an awkward massage from the very welcoming Dr. Mariszka back in Stockton-on-Tees?

"Now I just need your member number," the hostess says.

Ten seconds longer and Maria would have given a fake member number, but I'm not quick enough. We reveal that we aren't members and after some sincere apologies the hostess says that we probably should leave. We ask if we can exit through the walled garden. She tells us there's a way out at the far end that will take us to the road we need to find the main gate.

Who can say what impulse overtakes us at that moment? Defiance of authority? Class warfare? We take our time walking through the garden. Maria poses for pictures in posh wicker cabanas. We stroll through a greenhouse where they seem to be growing all manner of fruits and vegetables and spices, probably to be served up at dinner on the plate of some wealthy sheik from Dubai, who's only arrived six hours earlier. I take out my Laguiole knife—the Cadillac of French knives—and cut off a bunch of grapes from an arbor growing overhead. I shove them into my day bag and try to look nonchalant. I am stealing a bunch of grapes. I think to myself. It's a pointless act. I'm not even hungry. And I'm on pilgrimage.

We exit the walled garden and enter the small road that the hostess says will take us back to the main gate. Suddenly, a black SUV pulls up and stops. Another black SUV appears behind us. The grapes! is all I can think. Men in dark suits exit their vehicles and approach us from all directions. Before they say anything, I speak.

"Oh, thank goodness you're here," I say. "We're totally lost."

"You shouldn't be here," says a brawny man, as he adjusts his cliché dark sunglasses and identifies himself as part of the security detail.

"I know," I say. "We're so sorry. Can you point us in the right direction?" I'm sure they're going to escort us off the property and all I can think about are those damned grapes in my bag, but Mr. Dark Sunglasses simply points us down the correct road and admonishes us not to leave that road or divert from it until we hit the main gate.

Hearts racing. Close call. Maria and I laugh all the way home.

We arrive in the most adorable village of Luss, where we'll stay for four nights. Our original plan had us hiking to Tyndrum, much further north, but those plans have fallen through. Now, I can't imagine anything better than Luss.

We're in the Luss Pilgrimage Centre, which is basically bunk beds in three construction trailers, stitched together with some bathrooms at one end. The showers are hot, though, with good water pressure, so we feel we're in the lap of luxury. (Take that, Loch Lomond Golf Club!) We use what appears to be the church rectory for meetings and meals. There's a parlour with a working fireplace, around which we gather, telling stories about our lives, as the rain falls without relief.

18 August

It's Friday. The rain continues and we decide not to hike today. Al complains a little, but no one else. More time by the parlour fire. More tea and assorted biscuits from a tin and games of Scrabble and stories. And naps. The parlour feels like protected space, like a home for our family.

19 August

At breakfast this morning, Ann asks Chris if he knows how to use Photoshop. He does.

"Can you make me a picture?" Ann asks.

"Sure," Chris says.

"Can you make it so I look beautiful?" she says, "but in a way that reveals my *inner* beauty? I don't want you to change anything."

Chris tries to explain what he sees as the illogic of Ann's request.

"Photos don't reveal inner beauty," he says. "Photos only show what's on the surface. Only actions and behavior reveal inner beauty. And ... why do you want me to use Photoshop anyway, if you don't want me to change anything? I mean, the whole point of Photoshop is to change the photo."

Ann's eyes mist up and she leaves the room. Ann is already beautiful on the inside, I think to myself—one of the most beautiful people on the pilgrimage. She doesn't need Photoshop to show that, and she certainly deserves a better response than what Chris offers up.

"Well done, you," I say to Chris.

"What?"

"She doesn't need you to explain Photoshop, you numpty. She just wants some affirmation."

Chris is slow, but it does sink in.

The people are the pilgrimage.

In the evening, the congregation of Saint Kessog's Parish Church at Luss holds a special ceremony for us.

Saint Kessog's Church, Luss.

Brief congregational history alert:

> Saint Kessog—Celtic for "little spear"—was an Irish missionary who evangelized this area from his home base on Monks' Island in Loch Lomond. According to tradition, he founded the original church in Luss around 510 AD. Because of Kessog, Luss claims over 1500 years of continuous Christian presence in the region. The current church is much more recent, constructed in 1875. In 2001, the parish spent almost

£1M on restoring it. They got help from Historic Scotland and the Heritage Lottery Fund, but the community itself raised £100,000.

There are only 100 people who live in the village, with the entire parish consisting of just 400. Pilgrimage-inspired tourism (and probably regular old tourism) brings over 750,000 visitors a year to Luss. Their entire economy runs on pilgrimage.

Everyone of any importance in Luss is here: the vicar, the mayor, lots of community leaders. David has come down for the event. Saint Kessog is Church of Scotland, not Catholic. It seems like a big deal to have these "inter-faith" moments, like at Saint John Baptist, the Anglican church in Berksell. They do this sort of thing all the time back in Minnesota, at the very progressive Lutheran university where I used to teach. Here it seems like the wounds of the Reformation are still healing.

The event is intended as a welcoming ceremony, not a church service. Nonetheless, there are readings from the Bible, a bit of ritual from the book of *Common Order* and a hymn or two from the *Church Hymnary*. Words of welcome are spoken, and then I'm called upon to give a brief presentation about the Pluscarden 1230 Pilgrimage. Al has also acted as a spokesperson for the pilgrimage, as recently as a week ago. I remember his talk and crib most of the good parts.

After the ceremony, many of the village folk come up to welcome us with handshakes, questions, and encouragement.

12

Luss *to*
Stratherrick

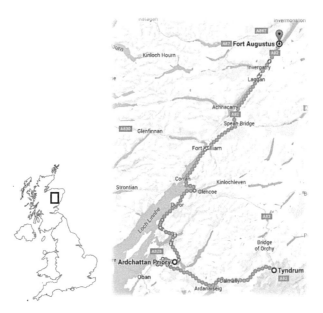

20 August

New pilgrims arrive. I recall from our time in France how we used to be concerned with integrating them into the group. Now "the regulars" feel like experts at welcoming the "newbies." The new pilgrims seem like they'll fit right in: John, Nick, Rosemary, and Sarah, the last of whom has special dietary needs, which makes Ann nervous.

John immediately tells several of us in the group that he's a recovering alcoholic and how visiting Pluscarden Abbey over the years has helped him. At least that's what I think he tells me. His Glaswegian accent is so thick that I can hardly understand a word he's saying. This wouldn't be so bad, except that I soon discover that John likes to talk, almost non-stop. He will become my own Margery Kempe. I can't recall why, but we start calling him "Glasgow John." He doesn't seem to mind.

"Aye, right," says Glasgow John. "A'm knackered. Best be off fer a wee kip." (Okay then. I'm exhausted, so I'm going for a little nap.)

The Spaniel has returned! Andy's first act upon arrival is to head to bed for a "wee kip" of his own. The idea of napping doesn't bother me at all when Glasgow John does it. I don't know how far he's travelled to join us. Andy is a different matter. None of us necessarily expect improvement from his behavior in France, but we all accept that he'll probably be with us until the end of the pilgrimage.

Because we didn't hike on Friday on account of the rain, Al suggests that we hike today. Remember, we aren't really getting from one place to another. Jai or Chris or someone will fetch us at the rendezvous point at the end of our hike and bring us back to the pilgrimage centre at Luss. This is about putting in the miles. Linear progress doesn't seem to be the measure of our pilgrimage, but overall mileage, even when there are fits and starts and gaps along the way. Since it's Sunday, a day of rest, Al devises a short walk of 10 miles along the West Highland Way.

The best part of this hike is the small boat ride we have to take to cross the loch and get to the start of the trail. As soon as we arrive, the light mist turns into light rain and these two weather patterns alternate throughout the day.

The path Al has chosen is arguably full of the most striking scenery we've encountered, but it's also the most treacherous in terms of terrain. You might pass out from sunstroke walking on a Roman road in the Champagne territory of France, but you probably wouldn't break any bones from the fall. This section of the West Highland Way, however, is basically a hike along the steep side of a mountain. There are small rivulets and waterfalls coming down the mountainside and cracks in the rock that you have to jump over. They aren't big jumps, but the ground is slippery from all the mist and light rain in the air. Many of the paths are only wide enough for one person, so it's tricky when you encounter someone coming from the opposite direction.

I'm hiking with Maria and Jo. They're easily outpacing me and I find it very kind that they stop and wait for me every so often. On easier terrain, they would have forged ahead, but they're watching out for me on this slippery slope. During one of our water breaks, Jo shares memories of making this same hike with her recently deceased husband and she tears up. I hope this pilgrimage is doing something for her grief. At the very least, she's taking opportunities to express it.

One of my problems on this hike is my rain gear. Rather than a sleek rain jacket that zips up close to the body, I've packed a large, hooded, forest green poncho. This looks fantastic when I'm walking in the rain alongside a canal. People tell me how I look more like a pilgrim than any of the others—especially using Angus's walking stick. These comments please me no end. I'm the slowest walker and I log the fewest miles, but I look the best. Pathetic. Even more pathetic is how impractical this poncho is on the slope of a mountain along the West Highland Way. It billows in the wind and obstructs the view when I try to find my footing. It's wet and rainy, so I don't want to take it off, but I have to wrap the poncho's loose ends around my waist to keep from tripping over it, which makes it less effective as a rain shield. I finally opt to take it off and drape it over the strap on my bag. I don't want it to get the inside of the bag wet, but none of that really matters because my entire person is soaked within the first hour of our walk.

We trudge on for a total of about four hours, but the going is slow and we aren't making good time. The others are probably done by now, but I don't think we've passed mile 6. After a long trek through mud that sticks to our boots and makes our feet twice as heavy, we come to a clearing that has a flagpole with an orange volleyball tethered to its pulley. This is the signaling device if you need or want a boat to fetch you from across the loch. We can see buildings there and a restaurant and other signs of civilization, so we raise the orange volleyball to the top of the flagpole. Within minutes, we see a small boat heading our way. For £5 each, it ferries us across. Best £5 I've ever spent.

From the restaurant on the other side, we phone Chris, who, as it turns out, has been sent to look for us and is not far away. The restaurant we're in is not as posh as the Loch Lomond Golf Club, but it's pretty nice. Maria and Jo and I are tattered and soaked and covered in mud. We don't care. We grab a booth and I order some scones and a cuppa, a side of chips, and a Coke.

Some day of rest, I think to myself.

21 August

It's the start of week 12. Only twelve days left in the pilgrimage and I'm done. I miss my dog. I miss my friends and my house. I start to feel a bit sad about having to say goodbye to my new family, but I'm ready. I can tell that I'm already packing for home in my mind.

At Mass this morning, Father Martin was putting on his habit in front of the gathered worshipers and he put it on backwards. We all giggled. He just shrugged. He often has these discombobulated moments, but he doesn't seem to have a mean bone in his body.

The entire walk today is along the heavily-trafficked A85 highway. It's dangerous and it sucks and this is also where we'll be hiking tomorrow. I find a path along a forestry road, but this is tricky because there are numerous lorries hauling logs to and fro and I'm afraid of getting too far off my map.

Evening comes and we find ourselves staying at the Craig Lodge, a Catholic youth community in Dunlaly. We're sleeping seven men in one room. The water in the tub is cold, but at least there are real beds and catered food in a cafeteria.

The Craig Lodge community celebrates Mass in the post-Vatican II style, with guitars and folk music during the Mass, rather than more traditional chants and hymn. The place is high energy because of the thirty or so students in their teens and twenties who are staying here for the summer, working and praying and living in intentional community. They're trying to do the same thing we're trying to do, but in one place, rather than on the road.

A beautiful young woman named Natasha, a sort of camp counselor in the group, has just adopted a border collie puppy that has similar markings to my border collie at home. She's playing with it in a courtyard and lets me join her. This takes away some of the edge from this morning's homesickness.

22-23 August

We compromise today and organize a shorter walk in the afternoon, away from the A85, in order to fit in a morning visit to the ruins of Ardchattan monastery.

It's raining again when we pull into Ardchattan. This is the first time I've visited the site, but I'm on my game and ready to give a lecture. A woman in her forties, the caretaker, must have heard us drive up and has come out to welcome us.

"Are you the professor?" she asks. I think back to meeting Ann in front of Canterbury Cathedral.

"Aye," says me. "I'm the professor."

She points us around the building to a gate where we should start our tour, then says that she'll have tea and biscuits for us in the lodge whenever we're done. With that she points in the opposite direction to a large building that must be the lodge. We find a spot with some protection from the rain, and I begin.

Expert lecture on the Order of Val-des-Choues no.1:

The Order of Val-des-Choues kept a giant ledger called the Grand Cartulary (literally, the big book of charters), in which they documented all of their economic transactions—donations, purchases, sales, etc. The Grand Cartulary recorded four of Val-des-Choues's daughter houses in Scotland, though it didn't name any of them. There are only three that we know anything about: Ardchattan, Beauly, and Pluscarden, all founded in 1230.

To understand why the monks of Val-des-Choues came to Scotland, we need to know something about a cleric named William Malvoisin. Around 1180, Malvoisin became secretary to King William the Lion of Scotland. This position gave Malvoisin lots of influence over the king. In 1199, William promoted him to Chancellor of Scotland. In 1200 he became bishop of Glasgow, then in 1201 transferred to the bishopric of Saint Andrews. When William the Lion died in 1214, Malvoisin enthroned his son as the new king, Alexander II, who in 1215 appointed Malvoisin Ambassador to England. That was a tough year for England what with King John being defeated at Runymede and the whole Magna Carta thing. As soon as he was appointed ambassador, Malvoisin made a brief visit to King John, but his real destination was Rome to attend the Fourth Lateran Council, a big meeting of all the top clergy in Europe.

Malvoisin wanted to reinvigorate monastic practice in Scotland and his excursion to Rome was a kind of shopping trip, to see which monastic orders might fit the bill. Traveling across France toward Rome, he encountered two new orders: the Dominicans and the monks of Val-des-Choues. The Dominicans were resolute preachers, Malvoisin must have thought, who could minister to the flocks in Scottish towns. As for the Val-des-Choues, they could build monasteries in the countryside and serve as an example of austere piety. Malvoisin brought this suggestion back to the king, who couldn't have

Ruins at Ardchattan Priory, Ardchattan, Argyll. Notice the carved skulls left and right of the arch.

been happier. In 1230, Alexander II founded four Dominican houses, one each in Edinburgh, Berwick-upon-Tweed, Ayr, and Montrose. In that same year, he established three priories under Val-des-Choues, Pluscarden in the county of Moray, Beauly in Ross, and Ardchattan in Argyll, where we find ourselves today.

We don't know much about the history of Ardchattan priory itself. In 1221, the lords of Argyll rebelled against the king and lost. As a consequence, Alexander II required Duncan MacDougal, Lord of Lorn, to hold his territories from the crown, making the MacDougal clan less independent. In 1230, it looks as if Alexander forced Duncan to found Ardchattan as part of negotiating the peace. A monastery in this part of his kingdom would give Alexander more influence in the western territories, in addition to serving Malvoisin's goals of bringing monks back to Scotland.

Ardchattan is located on the north shore of Loch Etive, northwest of Oban. The choir of the church is roughly 66 feet long.

Little remains of the rest of the church. The other monastic buildings have been incorporated into a modern dwelling, with the old refectory at its centre. You can still see some rib vaulting there.

I realize that what the caretaker has called the lodge is, I think, the old refectory. After some rainy looking about, we go to the lodge where tea and biscuits await us. Very kind.

After tea, the weather clears and we get dropped off (somewhere) for the start of our walk to Ballachulish, along the shore of Loch Linnhe. It's only a half-day's walk because of the visit to Ardchattan, along another highway, but this one doesn't seem as treacherous. A Polish priest named Father Andrew greets us at the Church of Scotland hall in Ballachulish. There are hot showers in the presbytery, but no rooms. I sleep in the vestry among the multi-colored priestly robes. Many of the men sleep in the church, among the pews.

23 August

We spend a second night in Ballachulish, walking during the day, but returning to our base camp at the church hall. Ann has seemed down for a couple of days now, so after dinner I tell a story casting her as the Oracle at Delphi, who tries to answer the same question for everyone: What is the meaning of life?

"God," says Jo.

"God," says Father Martin.

"Humans create meaning to explain their lives," says Al. "The meaning of life is a human construct."

This strikes a nerve, but good discussion follows.

24 August

One part of the pilgrimage I haven't yet mentioned is the generous corporate sponsorships we received. One company gave us bottles of water to keep us hydrated. Land Rover lent us the vehicle Jai used. Hamlyns of Scotland donated hundreds of portions of porridge. Therein lies a tale.

The individual packages of porridge were stacked one on top of another, in much larger boxes that took up a lot of space in the back of the van, where we had to fit all the luggage. Someone had the clever idea to repack the porridge, to get rid of the large, clunky boxes, and put all of the individually wrapped portions into two large, black plastic rubbish bags. This was a really good idea because you could just toss these large bags on top of all the other luggage. The method worked beautifully until one day, during our pre-departure cleanup, Father Martin, to be helpful, tossed the large, black plastic rubbish bags (believing they contained rubbish) into the bins. Jo made it all the way to the next lodging before realizing that the porridge was missing. Once Father Martin's helpfulness was revealed, she drove all the way back to the previous lodging and retrieved our porridge from the dumpster.

On the way to Spean Bridge, we pass through Fort William and see Ben Nevis, the UK's highest peak, in the distance. Hoping to impress him, I tell Al about how I walked to the top of it with my students, maybe four years ago. He nods his approval, but it's clear to me that he can run up and down Ben Nevis three times by the time I reach the summit once. The male ego is a fragile thing.

We're in a community hall in the town of Spean Bridge. The space has the feel of a basketball gym. The women sleep in the kitchen and adjacent rooms. The men pitch their sleeping bags across the polished hardwood floor. It's cold. The Spaniel discovers a vending machine that regulates the heat. One quid buys you fifteen minutes of heat. Andy puts in four quid, figuring that will warm the place up until we can get to sleep. No luck. The place does get warmer because the heat is generated from giant electric heaters attached high on the walls around the room. The heaters give off a loud buzzing sound that resembles a factory floor that requires industrial ear protection and a red glow that makes it feel like we're inside a submarine about to go into battle.

Bloody hell!

No one can sleep now, except Jai, who is snoring away, almost as loudly as the buzzing from the heaters. Some of us can't stop giggling at the absurdity of it all. Andy moves into the extra (handicapped) loo to try and sleep there. Who knows how we ever fall asleep? Most of us are still laughing about it next morning.

25 August

We walk through Fort Augustus on the way to Stratherrick, where we'll stay through the weekend. Maria and I talk about love and relationships, fear of commitment, growing old and fear of being alone.

It's a beautiful sunny day in Fort Augustus, a touristy village where kilts and tartan scarves are sold and the big activity seems to be watching the locks open and close. It's actually pretty cool to see ships pass through the series of five locks right in the centre of town from the canal that parallels the River Oich into Loch Ness.

Fort Augustus also has a very good ice cream shop. I sit next to a couple from Bavaria and get to speak German to them. I ask if they're having fun on their holiday.

"Of course," the wife answers. "Even when it doesn't seem like it at the moment."

Wisdom from the Black Forest.

26 August

Stratherrick is about 10 miles north of Fort Augustus. We're in a church hall that's on an isolated road. There's a rectory, but no priest, just a caretaker. Some of the women sleep there, as does Father Martin. The church hall has a small kitchen and the sleeping arrangements are cramped. We decide to walk to the Whitebridge Inn for dinner, which is about an hour on foot, but when you're a pilgrim, who cares. Jai brings a van to shuttle people back after dinner, though some walk in the dark.

Father Andrew, from Fort Augustus, has joined us for dinner. He'll stay at Stratherrick tonight and walk with us tomorrow. A professional clarinetist before his ordination, he has his clarinet and plays for us after dinner. Benny Goodman tunes. Two young children from an adjacent dining room hear the music and peek in at the door. I invite them in and they seem mesmerized by the clarinet. One of their parents shows up and explains that they're on holiday from Spain. He asks his children to sing a song for us, in exchange for the music they've heard. The boy and girl sing a folk tune in Catalan. Their sweet, sincere performance fills the room. I think this is all amazing, but Jo doesn't like it. She tells me she was hoping for a quiet time with the "family."

After the clarinet recital, we get into a passionate discussion about faith, divorce, and the Roman Catholic church. Jai loses his cool and yells at Father Martin. Who knows what baggage is being trotted out there? Many feel uncomfortable. To me, it seems like the regular curve or rhythm one expects at this point in a trip like ours. Sooner or later, the tension has to find a release valve.

Week 12 is done. The final leg of the pilgrimage begins tomorrow.

13

Stratherrick
to Pluscarden

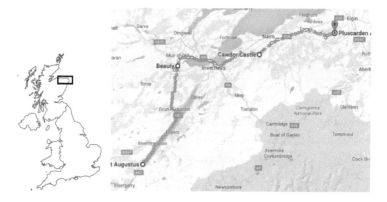

27 August

Final week of the pilgrimage. Four pilgrims leave us: Sarah, Rosemary, John, and Nick. Four more arrive: a new chap named Graeme, and returning pilgrims Lena, Richard, and Robbie.

Before departing, Nick reveals that he got a lot out of the trip. He's Mormon but enjoyed being involved in the "Christian debates" about faith and religion. He says that he mostly lives in an "RAF bubble" and he appreciated getting out of that for a while.

Ann, on the other hand, speaks to Al and me about her discomfort with last night's discussion, especially the raising of voices. She has a weepy moment but does not go into whatever feelings the loud voices of last night might have triggered.

This is the start of our last week. I try to give a little pep talk about how these final moments in a trip can become the most stressful, how people might express anxiety about transitioning back to our everyday lives. Father Andrew seems to approve, but Ann and Jo immediately get into a tiff over how the space should be put back together once we leave. It was quite a mess when we arrived, with tables and chairs and mattresses piled one on top of the other. We disentangled that mess when we got here and now the space, though still crowded, works better as a retreat house.

"Leave it as we found it," says Ann.

"Leave it as it is," says Jo.

One of them finally suggests asking the caretaker in the rectory, each one assuming, I suppose, that the caretaker will side with them.

28 August

Today, we walk the Great Glen Way. I rise early and help to reorganize the hall and pack the van before heading out with the walkers. Father Andrew and Lena and I seem to be at the rear of the pack. Lena is concerned that walkers should always be within sight of one another, even in the distance, so that there's less chance of getting lost. This is a good concept, but after a short while Lena forges ahead and we don't see her again until the RV point.

Father Andrew tells me his story of being kicked out of the Jesuits after 22 years. "Office politics," he says. True for every organization, I suppose. We stop on a bluff overlooking a valley to have lunch. As we're resting, Rinnes bursts forth from behind us on the trail, ecstatic to see us. Al and Graeme appear shortly thereafter and Al tells how Rinnes had been picking up a scent and knew we must be nearby. I'm a little confused about how we've gotten in front of Al, but a couple miles back there was a fork in the road offering the choice of an "easy" path, which Father Andrew and I have taken, or a "difficult" path, which Al and Graeme chose. It's the one and only time I find myself ahead of Al on the entire pilgrimage. But, hey, it's not a contest. Right? I mean, it isn't, unless I'm winning.

At some point Father Andrew decides to forge ahead. I'm once again last in the queue.

More than halfway along the Great Glen Way, I see a sign in the woods advertising tea, with an arrow pointing off the path. It's about that time, I think, and make a slight diversion. The tea shop is in a lovely cottage with a thatch roof and a warm cozy feeling inside. I learn that the warmth is generated by a kiln in the pottery studio connected to the tea shop. All of this is surrounded by woods, except for a small car park accessed from a long dirt road. I guess they can't depend on random hikers for all their business.

I have tea and fruitcake and tell the waiter about the pilgrimage. He then tells Rebecca, the potter (who is gorgeous), and she comes out of her studio to chat with me. After a while she invites me into the studio to watch her throw a pot. I'm reminded of that movie *Ghost*, with Patrick Swayze and Demi Moore, where they work a slab of clay together at a potter's wheel. At the time, I thought this was the dumbest thing I'd ever seen, but watching Rebecca do it, it's damned sexy. I want to buy something of her work, but I'm loathe to take on any stuff that I'll have to pack and carry back with me, especially anything breakable.

I go back to my pot of tea, still warm at my table. Two women come in and sit down. They also saw the sign on their hike. One of the women is celebrating her 60th birthday, so the waiter says that she deserves her coffee in a special birthday mug. She seems quite happy about this, then registers some disappointment when the waiter clears her table and she realizes the mug is not a gift. The gift was getting to *use* the special mug. Hmm. I whisper to the waiter that I'd like to buy the special mug for the birthday woman. He washes it out and wraps it up. She's delighted and thanks me several times. The two women leave. Meanwhile, the waiter tells Rebecca about all of this and she comes out of her studio, kisses me on the check, and gives me a gift, a little clay roundel with a blue-green glaze, about the size of a tuppence coin or a US half dollar.

Be generous and receive generosity. Be kind and receive kindness. I'm trying to resist the suggestion that there's something "magical" about this pilgrimage. I deny this with every skeptical bone in my body. But such events don't happen in my regular life. What's going on here?

The last stretch of today's hike is all downhill. I see the others below at the RV point, with Jai leaning against the Land Rover, the picture of duty. We ride north of Fort Augustus to the town of Cannich and the church hall of Our Lady and Saint Bean, a cousin of the famous Saint Columba of Iona. Upon arrival, we find the Spaniel asleep in the hall. Jo informs us that he's been sleeping all day. I don't see what he's getting out of this experience.

Meanwhile, Robbie is making noises that Beauly may not be worth visiting, even though I think it's key to the pilgrimage. It's one of the three daughter houses Val-des-Choues founded in 1230. We're going—end of discussion.

I sleep in a broom closet. This only sounds weird, unless you know that Chris sleeps in one of the extra restrooms. Both of us get a good night's sleep—no snoring, no disruptions. Chris calls the scene "blissfully surreal."

29 August

Just as we did with Ardchattan, we make a plan to visit the ruins of Beauly priory in the morning, then do a shorter hike in the afternoon. Like Ardchattan, I've also never been to Beauly, but I'm ready to give a good, well-researched tour when we get there.

Expert lecture on the Order of Val-des-Choues no.2:

A 17th-century chronicle claims that monks from Val-des-Choues "came out of France ... anno 1222," and that on 9 July 1223, John Bysset of Lovat founded the priory of Beauly. According to this chronicle, Val-des-Choues sent six monks and one prior to inhabit their new Scottish monastery. The priory of Beauly is located in the parish of Kilmorach, roughly sixteen kilometers west of Inverness. The name Beauly, from the French *beau lieu*, means "beautiful place." One of Val-des-Choues's priories in the county of Nevers also bears this name, as do several monasteries from other orders in France and England. The name fits the location on the north bank of the winding River Beauly, surrounded by mountains, moors, and forests.

The ruins of Beauly Priory, Beauly, Inverness-shire.

The size of the church at Beauly—150 by 24 feet—suggests that its community never grew much larger than the six monks and one prior who originally settled there. The ruins at Beauly have several features dating from the thirteenth century: the wall of the south chancel; the eastern nave, which contains three triangular windows, similar to those found at Pluscarden; the south transept; and part of the north transept. The church has suffered a good deal of damage over the centuries, once by lightning, but ultimately by the English Civil War.

That's the kind of presentation I would have given at Beauly, if—and I hate to say this—if not for Robbie.

We arrive in the town of Beauly about 10:30am. This gives people time to visit the shops and enjoy some pastry and a cappuccino at the Corner on the Square café. At 11, we gather at the entrance to the priory ruins. I'm ready to go, but I want to wait and give folks time to show up, in case they want to hear the talk. Most of the group is here and I'm about to start, when someone says, "Wait. Robbie's coming."

I wait, only to find out that Robbie is not alone.

"Phil," says Robbie. "This is John. I just met him in the pub and he's the local historian. He knows all about Beauly and can help you with your presentation." Hmm.

After six decades on the planet, I've figured out those areas in my life where humility is required. I'm not musically inclined. I'm no longer athletic. I'm a decent teacher and a decent friend, but even in these matters I have my deficiencies. One area in which I don't think about humility is my expertise in matters concerning the monastic order of Val-des-Choues. It still makes me giggle to say so, but I am the world's leading expert on these monks. This comes in part because I've spent over 25 years studying them, but also because no one else in the world has done so. I see no need to be humble about this, but I also don't feel the need to brag. It simply is. I'm the world's leading expert, mostly by default. And believe me, being the expert on such an obscure topic, I have perspective. I'm not curing cancer or bringing about world peace. I'm lucky that I get to study history for its own sake. It's an honor and a privilege that I don't take lightly and I know that lots of folks think it's silly.

All of that said, what the hell is Robbie doing bringing some guy he's just met in the pub to my talk?! "John knows all about Beauly and can help with the presentation?" Are you effin' kidding me?! Even though Robbie is trying to wind me up, I can't be mean to John, whom Robbie has just found in the pub, a pawn in his evil plan. Instead, I try to engage John.

"How do you know about Beauly priory?" I ask.

"I've lived here my whole life," John from the pub says.

"Have you read books about the monastery? Or maybe found stuff in the library?"

"No," John says without any shame.

"So, how do you know the stuff you know?"

"I just hang out in the pub and listen to people's stories."

This is taking up time. I cede the floor to John and let him say whatever he's going to say so we can get on with it.

"That building there," John says, pointing to a modern building east of the priory. "Before that building was built, archaeologists came and did some excavating. They found a whole basement that used to be part of the monastery. I was here when they were digging." Okay, I think to myself. Maybe John has something going for him.

"The archaeologists said this basement was part of the monastery's old bakery." Members of our group ooh and aah. This is actually kind of interesting.

"But I don't buy it," says John from the pub. "I think it was a safe room to protect the monks from Viking attacks. There's probably a secret tunnel that links the safe room to the church, over there." Here John points to the ruins of the Beauly church.

There's a problem with John's narrative. The era of Viking raids started in 793, with the attack on the monastery at Lindisfarne, and ended in 1012, during the weak rule of Aethelred the Unready. Some historians stretch the Viking period to 1066, when William and his Normans (Northmen) conquered England.

As you all know by now, Beauly was founded in the year 1230, a good 164 years after the Norman Invasion. I don't say any of this to John or to the rest of the group. I'm actually kind of embarrassed for John, since he could have tested his own theory by checking Wikipedia. Records for Beauly are scarce, but it's certainly possible that other forces may have attacked. The idea that the monks would build a secret safe room, however, seems rubbish. The basic defensive elements of castles (why should monasteries be any different) were outer curtain walls, moats and drawbridges and gatehouses, turrets and towers, and machicolations (overhanging holes in a castle wall from which you could drop stuff on the enemy). The safest space inside the castle was the keep. There were hall keeps of one or two stories and tower keeps (donjons) that could be several stories high. The keep's basement was used for storing food and arms, but generally not for hiding out. A monastery is not a castle, but I think some of the same defensive rules would apply. So, I'm sorry, John of the pub, but I think you're getting your history from Dan Brown novels.

I finally give my talk, but it's unfocused. I'm able to cite a few historical facts and point out some of the architecture, but none of it is very good. I'm riled. Local historian John has wasted our time and it's all Robbie's fault.

It's just before noon. I grab my lunch and some water and take off. I have my map, so I don't need to wait for the others to start walking. I need some alone time so I don't explode. I move at a fast pace. I really need to burn off some steam. This could have been a pleasant hike. Lots of Bronze Age menhirs (standing stones) dot the landscape. The weather is perfect and I spot lots of wildlife along the path. I'm just too angry to enjoy any of it.

Come on man! You've let Robbie get into your head and now you can't get him out. What happened to "I put that woman down hours ago" and all that? I'm angry, and I'm angry about being angry, and I'm angry that I can't seem to let go of my anger, and I'm spiraling and I can't seem to stop. After walking for about an hour, I get a wonderful, terrible idea. I'll devise a story where Robbie gets his comeuppance. Oh, yes. A revenge story. Something about a brilliant scholar who is tormented by a wicked troll. Yes, that sounds good.

I'm the last one to be picked up at the RV point. Everyone else is already in Munlochy, north of Inverness, on a farm that is now the home of the Black Isle Brewery. There's a bonfire and a fantastic meal and delicious Black Isle beer. We'll be sleeping in a covered structure on freshly laid hay, the most comfortable bed you can imagine because it conforms to your shape. And it smells good.

I don't enjoy any of this because I'm still stewing about the slam to my ego. I spend the entire evening separate from the group, watching from a distance. Chris comes over to check on me, as does Maria, but I blow them off. Jesus, Phil, let it go. But I just can't.

Then I see something that gives me hope. It's so subtle I'm amazed I even catch it. The Spaniel is clearing dishes and picking up after dinner. He's helping out and asking folks if they need something to drink or if he can get them anything else. This is the last image I remember before I fall asleep in the hay.

30 August

Cawdor Castle, Nairnshire.

Today we walk to Cawdor Castle. (Don't call it the "Macbeth Castle." The current owners hate that.) I walk by myself again, still focused on my great revenge story. I don't remember much else about the walk.

In the middle of the Cawdor forest, I run into a big group of pilgrims, Al and Robbie and Chris and the Spaniel and a few others. This makes me happy because I can just follow them into the castle for this last mile or so. I have my map and I know it's not far to Cawdor, but it's hard to orient in the woods and easy to get turned around. I'm right behind them when my boot comes untied and in the time it takes to retie my laces, they vanish. I call out but get no response. Suddenly, I lose my direction. I become geographically embarrassed. Then it starts to rain. Hard. Oh, come on!

When I finally make it to Cawdor, I discover that we're not sleeping in the huge castle but camping between a car park and what must be a swamp. It's still raining and the midges, Britain's version of no-see-ums, are everywhere. Others have complained about midges the entire time we've been in Britain. I've been immune until tonight. Tents have been pitched, but everything is soaked. I anticipate a horrible night's sleep.

Al comes to the rescue. We still have two days of walking to get to Pluscarden, but by car his home is only 90 minutes away. Would I like to go home with him, rather than sleep in a midge-infested swamp? Oh, hell yes. He's already called his oldest daughter to pick us up at a pub in town, where we're all going for dinner. There's a generally good mood at the pub, in spite of the crappy sleeping conditions that await. People are laughing and telling their daily adventures. Once again, I witness the Spaniel— let me start calling him Andy again—being kind and solicitous to his fellow pilgrims. Hmm. Something has happened for Andy, even if it took till the last week of the pilgrimage. He's still 18 and still goofy, but different somehow. He's achieved a kind of grace, enacted in his own way.

I watch Andy and the others sitting around the table, even Robbie, and I realize my story cannot be about revenge. It has to be about forgiveness.

"Do you have a story for us, Professor?" someone asks.

"Not yet," I say. "Tomorrow."

31 August

The night at Al's is perfect. A hot shower and clean sheets. Best of all, a warm welcome from his wife and daughters.

Today we walk to Logie, near Forres, west of Elgin, where we have an elegant dinner in a grand home. I spend the day working on my story, which I offer to you here.

Final story-time story from the Pluscarden 1230 Pilgrimage:

Long ago, in the Middle Ages, there was a scholar, a student of philosophy, who wandered from university to university. He wanted to learn all he could to become a master, so that he might someday teach. He studied at Paris and Bologna and Oxford and Cambridge and all the great schools. He knew the ins and outs of grammar, rhetoric, and logic, not to mention arithmetic, geometry, astronomy, and music. He had studied both Roman and canon law and was an expert in the theology of Augustine and Thomas Aquinas.

After many years of study, the time came for him to give his disputation. This was an intense ceremony in which all the masters from all the universities came together to administer a kind of oral exam. The hardest thing about this exam was that it was public, and anyone from the audience could ask a question, if they wanted to.

Without really understanding why, the scholar had made an enemy of a certain troll. This troll had been living under a bridge when the scholar first encountered him. He quizzed the scholar in the usual way that trolls do, before granting permission to cross the bridge. The scholar could easily answer any question the troll posed. This angered the troll so much that he started following the scholar around, popping up in classrooms or in pubs, wherever the scholar might be lecturing. The troll would ask the most outlandish questions, sometimes going into obscure detail on the topic at hand, sometimes going off the rails in directions that had nothing to do with the topic. Either way, it disrupted the scholar's lectures, but there wasn't much he could do about it.

On the day of his disputation, the scholar saw the troll lingering outside the great lecture hall. He steeled himself for whatever annoying questions might come. But when the disputation started, the scholar looked around and couldn't see the troll anywhere. He let down his guard. The masters began the examination and everything was going well. Suddenly, an ogre stood up in the middle of the room. He read from a set of questions that someone had written down for him. As you know, ogres can read, just barely, but their handwriting is atrocious. You've probably already guessed that the troll wrote the questions down and gave them to the ogre, hoping this would really throw the scholar off his game—which it did.

Right in the middle of the scholar's comparative analysis of Augustinian and Thomistic expressions of predestination vs. free will, the ogre stood up and raised his hand.

"Why can't mules have offspring?" the ogre asked.

Just as the scholar was contrasting the mystery of the Trinity (one God in three aspects) with the mystery of Christ's combined humanity and divinity, there was the ogre again.

"Why are there only five colors in a rainbow?"

"There are seven," the scholar said, and began to discuss light refraction, first discovered by the 13th-century Franciscan, Roger Bacon.

"In the word 'scent,' is the letter s silent? Or the letter c?"

"What?" Now the scholar was way off track and he couldn't find his way back. This happened over and over again. The troll had given the ogre a long set of questions, which he posed at the most distracting times. The disputation ended. The masters decided that, under the circumstances, they could not pass the scholar. He would have to wait a year to take the exam again and would not become a master and be allowed to teach until he passed.

The scholar felt embarrassed and depressed, but also furious. If he ever got his hands on the troll, he thought. You don't want to know what he thought. He looked high and low for the troll, whom he now referred to as his nemesis, without any luck. After a while, his angry quest began to take a toll. His body became sickly and his mind was turning to mush.

Then he remembered a story told to him by a wise old monk, one of his masters when the scholar was still a young student.

"Everyone has two dogs living inside of them," the monk said, "constantly struggling for dominance. One is the dog of anger. The other is the dog of forgiveness."

"Which dog wins?" the student asked.

"Whichever one you feed," the monk replied.

And so, the scholar forgave the troll and the ogre. The scholar's life didn't instantly become perfect. He didn't experience enlightenment or anything like that, but at least he felt that his load had gotten lighter. He got back on the path and began to learn again.

Around the table, there are smiles and sounds of approval and even some applause. Some of the pilgrims, those who have not been with us for the entire journey, appreciate the story without really understanding its background. Members of the family understand it on many levels.

"I don't get it," says Robbie.

I smile. Either he's incredibly dense (which I don't think he is), or he's trying to wind me up with the most convincing deadpan delivery I've ever seen.

Either way, Robbie, I choose to feed the forgiving dog.

1 September

Some of the walkers take off from Logie. Others drive to a parking lot on the other side of Forres where supporters of the pilgrimage will join us for the last 9 miles. Some of the pilgrims from the French leg show up, as do some of the monks. There's a group of children and teachers from the Mosstowie Primary School. Along the way, Scottish media show up. People carry the British and French flags and banners with the arms of the abbey. Father Giles runs up and down the queue taking photos. Al and Maria carry the stone from Val-des-Choues in a wicker dog basket, as if they were carrying Cleopatra on a sideways litter. David leads. I take up the rear.

Rinnes, Al and Maria lead the final leg of the pilgrimage, carrying the stone from Val-des-Choues.

By the time we arrive at Pluscarden's gates, there must be well over a hundred people in the procession. Pilgrims old and new pack into the transept of the church. I can't quite bring myself to go in. Too many emotions. Joy. Sadness. From across the lawn, I spot Father Dunstan, perhaps my best friend at Pluscarden. In addition to his white monastic habit, he's wearing dark sunglasses and a blue baseball cap with "New York" emblazoned on it.

"Good on, you," he says to me. "You made this."

I feel humbled.

"Lots of people made this," I say.

"Yes, yes. But you. *You* made it. All of this came out of *your* imagination. Did you ever think, when you were writing your dissertation on the strange little order of Val-des-Choues, that it would lead to this?"

It's the best affirmation I could wish for.

Inside the church. David welcomes the crowd and introduces Maria and Al, who present the stone to the abbot, Father Anselm. There are speeches and prayers and laughter and applause.

A tent is set up outside the church where barbecue and other summer fare is being served. Pilgrims from throughout the summer reconnect and share their personal testimonials of the experience. Chris has fallen in love with one of the other pilgrims. Maria says that she's "rediscovered her faith." Veronica, of the gigantic suitcase, says that it was a "life changing experience." Ann, our good and faithful cook, says, "Those three months changed my life."

Father Mark tells me that his camera has been returned! The person who found it scrolled through the images until they discovered a picture of the Land Rover with a magnetic sign indicating the "Pluscarden 1230 Pilgrimage." A little bit of googling and they knew where to send the camera.

I see Pete and the first words out of our mouths, almost simultaneously, are "Got any bread?" We laugh and give each other a big hug.

Tomasz is there, too, and we're genuinely happy to see each other. He looks good. The bags under his eyes are gone. He's not smoking (at least not in the five minutes we're together). He's smiling and he has color in his cheeks. I can't help but think these improvements have come about, in part, because he's away from the stress of the pilgrimage support staff. It sounds like he's been spending lots of time at the abbey, working on himself. He tells me he's been meeting regularly with Father Giles and seeking his advice.

"He's very wise man," says Tomasz. "I am good."

Good on you, Tomasz. Well done.

Meanwhile, Andy, formerly known as the Spaniel, continues in his newfound deference and service to others. I meet his mother and other members of his family. The mother tells me how much change she sees in her son and she thanks me.

"Don't thank me," I say. "I wanted to strangle him half the time he was with us." She laughs.

"I know the feeling," she says. "But you helped him. Everyone on the walk helped him."

I find David and we have a moment.

"Project Ivanhoe," he says, recalling the name of the hotel where we met and plotted in Rome.

"Project Ivanhoe," I say. "Thank you for this."

"Thank you."

In that moment, one of the pilgrims who was only with us for a week (I'm embarrassed that I can't remember his name) walks up and asks me to sign a copy of my book on the Val-des-Choues. Normally this sort of thing would be a huge ego stroke, it happens so rarely. But I don't feel egotistical in that moment. I don't think I feel anything. It's not numbness or indifference. It's more the emptiness that the Zen masters talk about. I feel at peace.

There are many more goodbyes and shared memories and congratulations. I say goodbye to Chris and Pete and Joe and many others. I don't remember saying goodbye or anything else to Robbie. Funny. I look around for Jai, but he's nowhere to be found. Al tells me that Jai has already gone—called a cab as soon as we got here. Mission accomplished, so move on? Tough time with farewells? Too bad. I so wanted to thank him for being the rock that he was the whole summer. None of this would have happened without him.

I thank Al instead, since he's standing right there in front of me. I thank him for his wisdom and his patience and his friendship. I thank him for teaching me so much. Another big hug.

This is a fabulous party that's got just the right tone of celebration and melancholy. It's also exhausting, so I start to head back to the dormitory, where I'll spend the next two nights before returning to the US. Walking through the transept again, I spot Angus.

"Wait right there!" I say to him.

I rush to my little cell where I've hastily dumped all of my stuff, grab Angus's walking stick and rush back to return it to him. In the church, I kneel before him, striking a pose like a medieval knight swearing fealty to his lord. I hold up the stick to present it to him.

"Angus," I say. "Forester extraordinaire. You made this mighty walking stick in the forest behind Val-des-Choues in Burgundy. When your time with us had passed, you entrusted it to me. I have carried it with me for the entire pilgrimage to Pluscarden. I have leaned on it, found balance in it, and even used it to fend off the dog of anger."

Angus doesn't know the scholar and troll story, so he looks confused about the phrase, "dog of anger."

"So, here is your stick," I say. "It has served me well and I thank you for leaving it in my care."

Postscript

I spend three more days in Scotland.

On Friday, the day of the great procession, I stay at Pluscarden. In the early evening, before Vespers, I give a talk to the monks in their chapter room.

Pluscarden Abbey, Morayshire.

This talk is my initial report on the pilgrimage. I tell them how I came to see the pilgrimage as an analog to the two expressions of monastic life: the hermit's life (walking alone during the day) and the communal life (living together in the evenings). Many of them nod in recognition. I tell them how "story time" came to the pilgrimage—the broken cooker and the slow pizza delivery, the rain and the *Canterbury Tales*. I tell them how pilgrims started to see themselves in these stories, and how the stories sometimes helped us mediate our problems, or at the very least, led to good discussions about some of life's big questions. I tell them about my "nemesis" and how I try to use the story of the scholar and the troll to work through my anger toward forgiveness.

I start to tear up and suddenly find myself weeping. Some of this must be from exhaustion and some of it is from a feeling of accomplishment. Mostly, I think, it's from a sense of gratitude. I thank the monks and I can hardly get the words out through my tears. They thank me, and I insist that I'm the one who should be thanking them. Afterwards, many of them come up and shake my hand or give me that awkward "monk hug," where each person holds the other by the shoulders and they gently bump heads.

"Good, Phil," Father Giles says. "Good."

On Saturday, I spend a quiet, contemplative day at Pluscarden. I attend the prayer hours, but otherwise I don't have much contact with anyone. In the evening, Maria fetches me and takes me to her home in Buckie, on the coast of the North Sea, where I'll spend the night.

Maria's house is remarkable. I've no idea how many bedrooms it has, but she raised ten children there, so there must be quite a few. With all of the books she's been collecting on the pilgrimage, naturally, she has a library. There are floor-to-ceiling shelves, but as I look around I don't see any place for her new acquisitions. Standing in the middle of the library, she smiles at me.

"Can you find it?" she asks with that impish smile she has.

Maybe it's the inflection in her voice. Or maybe it's that we know each other so well after our intense summer walking and eating and living together. I don't have to wonder or ask her what she means.

"There's a secret door?"

She smiles again. I find the door within a few seconds and she seems disappointed that it didn't take longer. The passage behind it doesn't lead to a donjon, but down a short corridor to the loo. It's still fun.

We go to dinner at a Chinese restaurant. Maria treats. We hardly talk about the pilgrimage the whole evening. We don't reminisce about our favorite moments. She asks me what it will be like to head back to the States.

"It'll be tough," I say. "It'll also be fine. I wish I had more time to transition. I fly back Monday and start teaching on Wednesday." She nods.

I sleep well in one of Maria's many bedrooms. The bed is soft, the sheets are crisp, the pillows are just right, and there's a fluffy goose-down duvet. This is the last time for a while that I'll be describing my sleeping arrangements, I think. Soon enough, I'll be back in my own bed. On Sunday, Maria drives me back to Pluscarden. We attend Mass then say goodbye, at least for now.

Because I have an early flight out of Aberdeen, Jo has offered to let me stay at her place, which is near the airport. Father Benedict, another Pluscarden monk, is also flying out early, so Jo picks both of us up on Sunday evening and delivers us in plenty of time on Monday morning. I chat with Father Benedict for a while in the airport lounge. He tells me about the conference he'll be attending. I tell him about the courses I'll be teaching. My flight gets called so we shake hands and part company.

Turning the corner on the way to my gate, I literally bump into Robbie.

You have a keen sense of humor, God. A very keen sense of humor.

Both Robbie and I look confused, like we're seeing something out of context. What must he be thinking in this moment? Then I wonder if I've been fair to Robbie in my telling of this tale, or if my own *mishigas* is clouding my judgment. Even if he and I haven't always hit it off, Robbie has certainly been a big part of the journey for many of the pilgrims, like Julia. He's made friends along the way and contributed to their experiences—and he kept coming back, logging many miles on the abbey's behalf.

It feels like minutes that we've been blocking each other's way in the airport corridor but it's probably only seconds. We both start to laugh awkwardly. Robbie explains that he's on his way to a family wedding. I tell him the obvious, that I'm flying back to the States.

"Okay," I say. "Cheers."

"Right," Robbie says. "Cheers."

If I haven't always seen the best in you, Robbie, chalk that up to my own blind spots. Maybe next pilgrimage ...

***

Since summer 2017, many of the Pluscarden pilgrims have continued to enjoy each other's company—hiking and eating meals together, around Scotland and even in the Czech Republic. They're planning another pilgrimage for 2021, this time to Rome.

Acknowledgments

Just like monks and pilgrims, writers sometimes work as hermits, sometimes in community. I was lucky to have a generous group of friends who read early drafts of this work and made many helpful suggestions. My thanks to Father Anselm Atkinson, Father Giles Conacher, Randall Davidson, Brother Michael de Klerk, Jan Jackson, and Alistair Monkman. Thanks also to the fellow pilgrims who attended the reading of an early draft at the home of Maria Byron. Finally, Peta Broadfoot, a professional editor, volunteered her time to critique my work. It's a better book because of her thoughtful comments, and I thank her.

]

PHILLIP C. ADAMO is a retired professor of medieval history. He is the author of *New Monks in Old Habits: The Formation of the Caulite Monastic Order, 1193-1267*; *The Medieval Church: A Brief History*, 2nd ed., with Joseph H. Lynch; and numerous scholarly and popular articles. He is currently a freelance writer living in Minneapolis.